How Are You Still Single?

Still Single?

Ashley Rodabaugh

Website: howareyoustillsingle.com
Twitter: @howareyoustill1
Instagram: howareyoustillsingledotcom
Facebook: howareyoustillsingle
Podcast: How Are You Still Single?

I dedicate this book to my Great Uncle Chuck who passed away a few months before I finished it. He always wanted me to bring home a guy.

Great Uncle Chuck: "You've got to slow down and let a guy catch you."

Me: "Uncle Chuck, I need a guy that can keep up."

CONTENTS

How Are You Still Single?

Introduction

It's official: I'm thirty-two and still single. On most days, that statement doesn't bother me at all. But when you're like me, there are always those moments. Usually with married couples or older adults. Usually because I live in the Midwest. You're at a networking event, meeting a new coworker, or going to a family gathering. You're alone, smiling and happy. People are confused—You're happy? You're smiling? But you're *single*. Yes. I know it's crazy, but you don't need a man to make you happy. Well, you *shouldn't* need a man to make you happy.

At all these events, I'm almost always asked about my husband.

"Oh, no husband? …. Your boyfriend?"

"Nope."

"Oh…"

There it is. The sound of pity. The sound of judgment. Then it's followed by a question of utter bewilderment. As if saying I'm single is the most confusing thing they've heard in a while.

"But, *how*? How are *you* still single?"

Sometimes they add in a few backhanded compliments.

"I don't get it. You're so pretty, smart, and fun."

Now, I know what they're trying to say is I'm a catch. That guys should want to date a woman like me. What I hear, though, is:

"There *must* be something wrong with you."

Ouch. What I want to say is, "I've tried. I've dated. There is nothing wrong with me. Dating is just hard, especially now. It's not that easy." I want to tell them all about the terrible dates I've had and the guys who decided they didn't want to date me. So, I decided to write this book. To tell my story. To tell all those judging us out there what it's really like for some people when you ask us, "How are you still single?"

We ask ourselves that same question. I want to put you in our shoes. I want you to just try and understand why we hate getting asked that question. I want you to understand that although this is my story, I'm not alone. There are many others that have very similar stories. Both men and women. So, cut us some slack. And when we tell you we're single, stop asking us…

"But, *how*?"

You see, most single people have dated throughout their lives and for whatever reason, it hasn't worked out. Most people are surprised to find out that I wasn't the one to end almost all of my relationships. The guy usually broke up with me. Each time, it hurt and made me feel like a failure. I never wanted to share the fact I was single once again with my friends who easily found relationships and never seemed to have a hard time staying in one. I didn't want them to judge me for being single.

I am proud of the many things I've accomplished in my life from travels around the world to great friendships. There is so much more to life that makes you who you are than your relationship status. I hope this book helps others feel the same way. Follow me from my prepubescent, passing-notes, dial-up days in grade school through high school, onto my more serious relationships in college, grad school and into the adult world. They all start off just like all relationships should, but somewhere it goes wrong. I talk about all the unsolicited advice people in relationships tend to give those who are single. You know:

• You're not trying hard enough; you need to get more involved with things and then you'll meet someone.

• You're trying way too hard, just live your life and when you're not thinking about it that person is going to come along.

• You're just way too picky. You need to give more people a chance.

• Have you tried online dating? It worked for my friend.

These nuggets of advice are some of the most annoying things I hear when I tell someone I'm not in a relationship. I explain how I've told myself those same things and did them. Meet all the guys I've met as I followed all of the advice above in different aspects of my life. All of the guys come in, out, and back into my life, because even when they're the ones to end it, they always come back.

You'll meet TheOneYouMeetWhenYou'reNot-Looking, TheNextDoorNeighbor, TheOneYour-FamilyWantsYouToMarry, and ultimately end at TheOne. There's quite a lot of them so feel free to refer to the index in the back to help you keep them straight. I hope the names remind you of the people you or your friends may have dated, too.

I learn something from each one, but still usually end up confused as to why our relationship ended. Then I met TheOne who finally showed me everything I was looking for in a man. I hope, whether you're single or in a relationship, you feel my pain, laughter, struggles, and love as I take you through all of the relationships that led me to my thirties. I want you to discover or commiserate with me about how hard dating can be for some people. How we pick ourselves up and put ourselves out there over and over, again. How we want it to work out just as much as you want it to work out for us.

Here's to love and to all those still on their journey to find it. Thank you for buying my book! I hope those of you who have always had it easy finding a relationship learn a little bit more about what it's like for your single friends. I hope those of you who are still single learn you're not alone and love has a lot less to do with following methods and more to do with luck. Here we go…

1|Elementary/ Junior High School
(If You Can Even Call That Real Dating)

There's always that one couple in your life who found their one true love in middle school. Middle school. Straight up nose-picking, passing-notes, can't-even-drive-yet middle school. How? How is that even possible? And they're still actually married ten, fifteen, twenty years later. I can only assume it's pure luck, or perhaps they never truly grew up since then so they're basically the same people, but now they can drive and hopefully still don't pick their nose.

These are the people that will never understand why you're single and thirty. Never. To them, they just happened to find the right person in middle school. Most likely on the playground at recess, or they sat next to each other in the classroom. It was easy. One of them asked the other to be their girlfriend or boyfriend, the other said yes. Boom. Together forever. Most people relate to situations based on how they went through them. So for these couples, how the relationship started out was quite easy (even if they've had struggles since then). These people don't know what rejection feels like, nor do they have advice on how to deal with rejection from jerks (that's what I would call them in middle school—I must say my language has grown exponentially more profane as I've grown older).

Middle school was the first time I acted on my feelings for a guy. It was also the first time I felt rejected. Not only rejected, but full-blown smack-across-the-face rejected at the mere age of twelve. Looking back now, I realize it was the present giving me a glimpse into my dating future. What do they call it in literature? Foreshadowing. If only I had realized it at the time...Who am I kidding? Even if I had realized it, I don't think it would've changed a thing in my dating life.

LilBowWowWannabe

Now I had my fair share of crushes before the age of twelve. The names of those crushes were merely written in my childhood diaries and shared (by secret code name) with my friends through passed notes in class. I never acted on any of those crushes. They were merely contributions to my childhood imagination and gossip. Then I met LilBowWowWannabe. Obviously that's not his real name. Although, I'm sure at that time he would have loved to have been called Lil Bow Wow. I'm pretty sure his Yahoo Messenger name was some derivative of LilBowWowWannabe.

Yes. This was the age where dial-up internet was starting to be used. For those of you too young to remember, dial-up internet required the use of a phone line to hook up to the internet. If you were on the internet, the phone line was busy, and no one could call through to your house. As you were getting on the internet, it took a good fifteen-to-twenty minutes to connect. The connection always had the most annoying sound to notify you that the internet was attempting to dial in to the phone line.

EEEWHheewAAHHHHeeeeeeHHaaaHHWWWeeeeeee

My phonetic interpretation of the annoying internet sound.

Along with dial-up internet came the online instant messenger programs that allowed you to create names and profiles to talk to other people from your school. My "romantic" junior-high relationship developed from this messaging tool. However, even back then, words could be misread and misinterpreted when typed out on a computer or sent through a phone.

Besides the fact that the name "LilBowWowWannabe" is a derivative of this guy's messenger name, he also somewhat believed he was just as cool as the rapper Lil Bow Wow. This small-town Ohio white guy who went to a catholic private school thought he was a "gangsta." I, in my awkward, immature period of life, bought into this "gangsta" attitude. He was just too cool for school. (On a side note, I can't say too many bad things about this guy. He fought and overcame childhood cancer. So, even though I wouldn't consider him a "gangsta," I for sure consider him a badass for overcoming such a huge battle at such a young age).

LilBowWowWannabe and I started off as friends. We would have fun at our friends' parties (I'm talking water-gun fights, swimming, playing sports—not drinking, come on now! My dad was way too overprotective to let me get away with that, especially in middle school). We seemed to have fun together and he liked to message me a lot on Yahoo Messenger. As we hung out more and more, I started to like him more and more. I decided I wanted him to be my boyfriend. You know, just like those couples I mentioned earlier. I tell you I like you. Boom. We're together. That's what I wanted.

Now, I'm not sure if it's because my parents raised me to be an independent thinker or I was just a stubborn person who never really listened to many of society's rules, but for whatever reason, I decided *I* needed to ask *him* out. I wasn't going to wait around for him to pose the question to me. Going into this, I really didn't see that anything bad could come of me asking him to be my boyfriend. Especially since he seemed to be really interested in me.

I decided it needed to happen in person. This way, I'd have an answer right away, and I'd be able to see his facial expression (he's totally going to be smiling with excitement, right!??). Now, the timing had to be right, too, a time when we were having fun and would have the opportunity to see each other and spend some one-on-one time together.

Unfortunately, what I thought would be good timing and a great opportunity was, in retrospect, pretty bad timing. I decided to ask the question during a school dance. This dance was for both seventh- and eighth-graders and included students from multiple catholic schools in the area. (Super private location to ask, right? What was I thinking?). This was the last dance of the school year during the last month of the school year. Summer break was just around the corner, and I knew I had to ask him before then.

I dressed up in my dance attire (cute jeans and a branded T-shirt—such a hot outfit) and did my hair. Looking back at pictures, I was not good at doing my hair. Not at all. I had put it half up with some sweet-ass mini butterfly clips. I was dropped off at the dance with some of my other friends. (Oh yeah! Parents taking you to the party!). I spent the first half of the dance gathering up the courage to ask him and looking for reassurance from my friends that this was a good idea. My friends encouraged me, but I think more so just to see what would happen rather than thinking there was going to be a positive outcome.

Step one, I gathered up the courage to ask LilBowWowWannabe to dance for a slow song. We for sure didn't do any of that fast-song grinding kids these days do at junior-high dances. Nope. The slow song dances were done with the girl's straight arms awkwardly on the guy's shoulder and the guy's straight arms awkwardly on the girl's waist, both players keeping as much distance between each other as possible. At this time, you're still not sure if the whole guys-have-cooties thing is completely untrue.

He said, "Yeah we can dance." We then proceeded to awkwardly dance, swaying to the music and talking. I was still debating whether it was a good idea while the song started to wrap up.

(Tip: Listen to your gut!)

I told myself, *It's now or never*, and I didn't want to have regrets that summer of never asking and never knowing his answer. So I shyly asked (and I'm not shy), "Hey, LilBowWowWannabe, would you want to go out with me?" My heart was racing at this point, and I was starting to sweat with anxiety. He responded, "No." I was crushed and embarrassed. His friend— we'll call him JackAss —apparently overheard our conversation and thought it was the most hilarious thing he had heard. Yeah, how funny it is to get rejected. So. Freaking. Hilarious.

I don't remember much of the rest of that night. I quickly ran to my friends and found a way home and away from the situation. Welp, I had tried and failed with my first potential relationship. I was rejected and embarrassed. I wish I could say it ended there. I wish I could tell you the school year ended, summer started, and I went back to my normal junior-high life. Unfortunately, that is not what happened. Nope. This form of rejection was not going to let up on me just yet.

I spent the weekend brushing off the rejection and acknowledging that dating LilBowWowWannabe was just not in the cards. I assumed school was going to be a little awkward on Monday, but I only had a couple more weeks left until the summer. I could easily ignore LilBowWowWannabe until then, and I was very good at ignoring people back then (immaturity at its finest). I figured I could for sure get through this with no problem. Little did I know that LilBowWowWanna-be's friend, JackAss, was not about to let me off so easily.

Monday rolled around. I snoozed my alarm per usual and rushed to get ready and out the door in time for my bus. I had already taken a shower the night before in order to snooze my alarm as many times as possible and expedite my getting ready-time in the morning. Unfortunately, sleeping in wet hair all night doesn't do much for your hairstyle in the morning. But this was junior high, sleep was a much higher priority for me than my hairstyle.

The one good thing about not being a morning person and rushing around is that I have no time to think about things. I can only think about what I need for school that day. The only thing on my mind was making sure I had my homework to turn in and all the books I needed for school. I wore a uniform, so that didn't require much thought to get ready. Despite the lack of choices for dress, I still managed to barely make it out in time for my bus to pull up.

I boarded the bus and started chatting with some of my friends. I took the public school buses to school. Since we didn't attend the public school that owned the buses, we were the last to be dropped off. We also had to switch buses midway on our route to school so all the private school kids could be funneled onto one bus from all the public school buses. Due to this, we usually took an hour to get to school. The long bus drive allowed my mind to wander. By the time I got to school, my anxiety of running into LilBowWow-Wannabe was starting to grow.

I went through the first few periods of the day, and everything seemed to be back to normal. Most people were more concerned with their own lives than caring about what happened in mine, no matter how embarrassed I felt about it. Lucky for me, it seemed like most people had completely forgotten or never heard about what happened between LilBowWowWannabe and me at the dance.

Then it was time for science class. My school was very small. We had around sixty students in our seventh-grade class, maybe fewer. We all knew each other; and we all knew about each other's business. Our science classroom was set up with long black laboratory tables and blue plastic chairs set up behind them. The class was always right after lunch, so our teacher was often a little later than the rest of us.

I was reluctant to go this class. LilBowWowWannabe was in the class with me and I sat right in front of him. And sitting next to LilBowWowWannabe? His friend, JackAss. I walked into the classroom attempting to avoid any eye contact with either of them. I figured if I didn't look at them, then they wouldn't notice me. I quickly scurried to my seat and slid behind the table. I noticed our teacher wasn't there yet. Never a good thing. The boys were much more likely to say or do something without the teacher there. No way for them to get into any trouble.

Just as I sat down, I heard JackAss's voice. All I could think was, "Oh no, here we go." He said as loudly as he could, "Hey, Ashley? Remember when you asked LilBowWowWannabe Out and he said NO!?" He and the rest of the class, who I didn't even notice had taken their seats, burst out laughing while staring at me. All of them were laughing, including LilBowWow-Wannabe. Awesome.

I wanted to crawl up into a ball and slowly inch out of the classroom. I wanted to be anywhere but there. I was beyond embarrassed. Luckily, the teacher came in just a minute after he mocked me in front of the whole class. He asked why everyone was laughing. Of course, no one would admit anything. I was happy it was over and we could concentrate on Science. I was also relieved knowing I only had a few more weeks to deal with either of them. I never wanted it to be summer break more than that year.

Well, there you have it. That was my first chance at a relationship. You can tell me I did it wrong. He should have asked me out, and not the other way around. Maybe you're right. (I still disagree—why does it always have to be up to the guy?) But after that embarrassing ending, it would take years before I ever told a guy I was interested in him before he told me. So to those who married the first person you dated, it's not always that easy. Sometimes the person tells you no and you get publicly shamed for even attempting to date them. Sometimes it's not all unicorns and rainbows. Sometimes it really, really sucks.

Now, I wish I could tell you I learned my lesson. I wish I could tell you that I most definitely wasn't going to date LilBowWowWannabe ever. Never ever. I can tell you that was what I thought was going to happen as I left my school for summer vacation. I thought I would never want to even be his friend. Well, unfortunately, I like to learn lessons the hard way. Always. Not only would I learn this lesson the hard way, but I would learn many more throughout my dating life the hard way. Hopefully it will pay off one day.

The summer flew by. I went to summer camp and on vacation, and soon I was back at cross-country practice and school was upon me. Luckily, stories of vacations and other drama occupied the gossip of the school, and my embarrassing rejection was no longer the topic of conversation. I'm also not one to hold a grudge. Plus, when you're in a small school, you're kind of forced to get over things. You will see everybody in your class. It's hard to avoid anyone.

Both LilBowWowWannabe and JackAss seemed to have moved on from making me the center of their ridicule, too. By the end of the eighth-grade school year, I had actually become friends with the both of them again. By the end of the year, LilBowWowWannabe seemed to be sending me signals that he was interested in dating me. At first, I didn't believe it. No way. I had already misread those signals once; no way was I going to do it again. I played along with the signals, but I never acted on anything.

Then that seventh- and eighth-grade dance came around again. The same one, with all the students from all the catholic schools in the area. The same small gym. I wore a very similar outfit. This time *he* asked *me* to dance a slow song. By this time, we had become very good friends. I didn't think anything of him asking me to dance. We talked and slowly swayed back-and-forth. This time, he seemed to be the nervous one. I thought he was being a bit odd, but who knows—maybe he's just nervous slow-dancing with girls?

The song started to come to an end, and I started looking to see where my friends were to catch up before the end of the dance. Then *he* asked *me* if I wanted to date. What? What is going on right now? Oh, how the tables have turned a year later. A couple of thoughts went through my head. *Now it's my turn to reject him! Now it's my turn to let him experience rejection and know how it feels to be embarrassed*. But then I remembered how much that sucked for me. Why would I want someone else to go through it? *An eye for an eye* never resolves anything; it just leaves you both blind.

Instead, I said yes. What the hell, I had fun with him. I had never had a boyfriend before. I was excited, even though I still didn't really know what it actually meant to be boyfriend and girlfriend.

We continued to be boyfriend and girlfriend for about a month. That was a long time for eighth grade! I mean, way longer than a day or week. Woo-hoo! He was also my first kiss. It wasn't anything special. In fact, it happened so fast, I'm not even sure he made contact. We were at a friend's bonfire (that's what you do for fun when you live in rural Ohio). I went to leave, and he gave me the fastest peck on my lips I ever had. He broke up with me shortly after that. Something about wanting to be single in the summer. You know, because the summer going into high school is so happening.

The breakup didn't really bother me too much. It was sad, but I had another summer filled with trips, camps, and I was about to go into high school. All in all, it wasn't a bad experience, but he certainly wasn't the love of my life. He was just one stepping-stone in my search for a guy who could be my partner in crime. For some, their love stories begin here, but for most, it's just the beginning of a journey to find their own love story.

2|High School

(When You Think You're Older Than You Are)

High School. The best days of your life. Well, that's what some people will tell you. High school, for me, was definitely *not* the best days of my life. They also weren't the worst. They were just days in my life. Days when I grew and learned and always yearned for the future—for college.

High School started off….interestingly. I went to a small catholic school with fewer than 400 people combined. My class graduated fewer than 100 students. Our school was set up in an X shape (or maybe it was supposed to be a cross-like shape? It wouldn't surprise me…). Either way, each of the four halls/wings was designated for a specific grade. Your locker was located in that hall for the entirety of the year; then you'd be moved to another wing, a sign of moving on up.

On my first day of school, the senior boys surrounded the hallway where the freshman lockers were located, forcing us to walk through them before we could go to class. They would judge our hotness out loud as we walked by. "Oh yeah…look at her…I'd hit that." "Ewww…no way!"

I happened to walk through as the school bell rang, so I don't know the outcome of my assessment—luckily. I'm sure many of the other girls took their comments to heart and carried them in their thoughts for the next four years….if not longer. High-schoolers are cruel. Hell, most kids can be cruel. Words meant so much to us back then, sometimes even now. I survived my first day. Survival was my goal. Make it through the next four years and then I can leave. Leave for greener pastures. Leave for the college life.

In high school, I had a strong personality—let's face it, I still have a strong personality. For the most part, I didn't care what people thought about me. Again, I was leaving this place. Most guys were (still are) "intimidated" by me. Well, that's what they would tell me anyway. High school was a means to an end for me. My goal was to get through school with good enough grades to go to a college far, far away from high school. A school located in a city that didn't care if you played for a division-three high school football or basketball team. (Division three, for crying out loud!) A city where I could be whatever I wanted to be, and it didn't matter if my family had already made a name for me. Where I could make a name for myself.

Finding a man was not one of my high school goals. Sure, I had my crushes, but I didn't have a goal to find a boyfriend. I didn't think my friends had that goal, either, but then all of a sudden, my close friends were suddenly paired up. Woah! That was fast! Like, really fast. All of a sudden, I was fifth- or seventh-wheeling it to movies and hangouts. Little did I know, this was just practice for many years of joining couples on trips, movies, you name it—I was the single one.

Now, to be fair, I'm a very hyper-active person. I can't really sit still for very long. Actually, I'm surprised I've managed to sit still long enough to write this book. I constantly need to do something. Anything. So in high school, I danced, I cheered, I played soccer, and I attended any and every camp I possibly could during the summer. So needless to say, my friends had a lot more time to think about and actually date a guy. I, on the other hand, had a hard time fitting high school social time into my extra-curricular schedule. But those activities were my outlet from the day-to-day drama and straight-up bullshit that was high school. They distracted me from the petty gossip and kept me on my goal of leaving for college.

Back to my friends. I only had a handful of close girl and guy friends in high school. I didn't care about being in the so-called popular crowd. Most of that crowd didn't really want to be my friend, anyway. So, I stayed close with the few that were genuine. We're still friends to this day. So that small group of friends had been sought-out by a group of junior boys. Those boys had measured up all the freshman girls and set their eyes on my friends. They pursued them and won them over. I was not one of those girls they pursued. There's also a small chance I was oblivious to any pursuit. Anyway, soon my friend-hangouts were friend-and-my-friend's-boyfriend hangouts.

Mr. Wimpity-WimpWimp

Now as juniors, these boys could drive and had cars to drive. (Not the nicest cars… we're talking old, beat-up, used two-door cars—but they could drive). They could pick us up and take us to the mall or the movies or to get ice cream. They showed us what it was like to have a little more freedom. It wasn't hard to persuade me to hang out with them all. I got free rides home from school. (I rode that beautiful yellow school bus until junior-year of high school otherwise…stupid school buses). They drove me to football games and to grab food. It was great for me. Well, as you hang out with the boyfriends, you also hang out with the boyfriends' friends. And that's how I met Mr. Wimpity-WimpWimp.

So you're probably thinking—ouch. That's a bit harsh of a name; maybe that's why it didn't work out. Well…let me tell you exactly how this so-called high school relationship played out. Maybe then you'll agree with me.

Mr. Wimpity-WimpWimp was a junior and friends with my friends' boyfriends. I hung out with him quite a lot. He was a nice, quiet, tall blonde. We were attracted to each other, but more so because we were two of the only single people in the group versus that movie-like romantic feeling. We started to get to know each other more by chatting online. As you'll see, the internet has played a large part in my dating-life.

As we grew closer and our friends' relationships grew stronger, it seemed inevitable that we would soon make our relationship official. This time, though, I was waiting for him to ask *me* out. I wasn't taking any more chances asking the guy out (see Chapter 1: "Elementary/Junior High School"). Then one day, it happened. He asked me to go out with him! Yay, right!? Except he asked me to date him via Yahoo Messenger. Hence, Mr. Wimpity-WimpWimp. Don't worry, though, he does more to earn his name.

I said yes to his question and nervously prepared to see him in person. Now at the time, I didn't even question if the person behind that screenname was anyone other than Mr. Wimpity-WimpWimp. Thankfully, he was indeed behind that screenname and asking me that question. But thinking about it now, he had three siblings, and really anyone could've been asking me that question—that could've been real awkward…

Anyway, the next day at school went well. We had both now openly acknowledged our feelings to each other, and they were actually mutual this time. I was able to go on real dates with him since he drove. We would go to the movies and just go driving sometimes. (Remember, this is middle-of-nowhere Ohio. We didn't have that many options!). He shared with me his music interests, mostly punk-rock. I still think of him a little when I listen to it now. We dated for about a month and shared a handful of very awkward kisses. I'm going to chalk that up to us just being new at the whole thing.

So a month in, I'm thinking things are going pretty well. I have nothing to complain about. My friends and I are all able to hangout with our boyfriends since they're all friends. We were most excited to attend prom together. In my high school, you had to be a junior or senior to attend, *but* you could go if a junior or senior invited you as his/her date. My friends and I were all excited to be freshmen and invited to go with our older boyfriends. I remember fantasizing about getting my dress and going with everyone. Too bad most of my fantasies remain just fantasies—even to this day.

So there I am, thinking everything is going well. I'm sitting at my computer at home and chatting with my older boyfriend on Yahoo Messenger. Then all of a sudden he types, *I need to talk with you about something.*

Uh-oh. When someone says this, in most all situations the "something" they want to talk with you about is not a good thing. So I respond, *Okay. What do you want to talk about?*

And this is why I decided to call him Mr. Wimpity-WimpWimp. He types: *I don't think we should be together anymore.*

No explanation. No face-to-face conversation. Nothing. Just a freaking Yahoo Messenger message. Looking back, I'm not sure how I could've expected more from him. I mean, he did ask me out on Messenger, too. I signed off quickly. Meaning he couldn't send me any messages. It's how I tend to deal with situations like that. Evacuate. Leave. Sign off.

I didn't want to see him at school the next day. I didn't want to talk to him. He didn't give me any explanation. I didn't understand why. I avoided him. To the point of speed-walking into the women's restroom. *Speed-walking.*

My friend told me Mr. Wimpity-WimpWimp wanted to talk, because he thought he made a mistake. *Yeah, buddy. You think?* All I could think was, *Yeah, I made a mistake, too. I made the mistake of dating him.* This will be a huge theme in my dating life. A guy ending a relationship with me. Me taking it as an actual end. The guy coming back (usually not the very next day) and me not believing he's changed and often refusing to give him a second chance.

There it was. My first high-school relationship. It started the same way it ended—in the world of Yahoo Messenger. Mr. Wimpity-WimpWimp never had the guts to talk to me in person. He wouldn't be the only one, but he was the only one to ask me out online and breakup with me online. My so-called relationship was over, and so were the friend-boyfriend hangouts. So was the freshman-year prom fantasy.

I cried it out and I turned my focus back to my extracurriculars. I was done with guys. I was done with Yahoo Messenger. I was back to focusing on the end of high school, until…my junior year.

MyPrecious

My junior year was the beginning of serious college prep. I was studying for the college entrance exams and trying to raise my GPA, write my personal story for college applications, and score some scholarship money. Then, one day, I got a phone call from a close friend.

"Hey Ash! Did you know MyPrecious has a crush on you?"

My response? "MyPrecious? Really? But, I don't even know him. We don't even really talk."

MyPrecious was on the football team and wasn't in most of my classes. At this point, I was in mostly honors class (again, college, college, college). He was in the general classes (football, football, football). We rarely saw each other. I found this to be odd. How could this guy like me or want to date me when he didn't even know me? He wasn't even a thought in my mind. I knew his name and what he looked like more so because we went to a really small school. I knew everyone's name in my class.

So I thought about this. Should I find out more about this guy? Should I let him take me on a date? I finally decided I would let this happen. Why? (And this was honestly my thought.) Well, he liked me, obviously. He liked me to the point where he had his friends tell me he liked me. So I figured, well…if it didn't work out, I could just end it. I wouldn't really get hurt because he's the one that likes me. (Wrong. So wrong. You'll see later).

So, I told my friend I would give it a try. MyPrecious: a name given to him by his friends after he started dating me. I found out about it after we had broken up. Did I mention High-schoolers are mean? A lot of his friends, behind my back, called me Gollum. You know that creepy creature from *The Lord of the Rings*? The one with thin, stringy black hair who's obsessed with finding the ring? Calling the ring "my precious?" Yup. Gollum. That's what his friends called me. Why? Well, obviously it's because they're idiotic, immature boys. Their reasoning? Because I had huge eyes, just like this creature. (If you don't know what I'm talking about, you need to Google that shit right now. Put down your Kindle. Close your book.)

I will say, one of them did apologize to me later. He called me when I was in college to tell me he felt terrible for making fun of me. Although it was nice to hear, I had long forgotten about those comments and those people. I had moved on to people who didn't call me names and quickly forgot about those haters. If you're going through the same thing right now, try your best to ignore it. It all will soon be in your past, those haters and their hater comments.

Anyway, so they called me Gollum, and my boyfriend? He was "my precious." *Rolling my eyes big time.* He was actually not a bad guy at all. He had a good heart and treated me well. I learned a lot from our relationship. Like, apparently you celebrate one-month anniversaries. Who knew? He would take me on actual dates. In fact, those were more serious dates than I've had since high school. Sadly. I think courting a woman has gone out the window. Hopefully it comes back.

He was one of the older guys in our class and had a car. A red Pontiac Grand Am. So. Hot. The hottest part of him driving me, though? He *always* opened my door for me. Both when I was getting in the car and getting out. His dad raised him right.

He was the only guy I've ever dated during my birthday. He was the only boyfriend to celebrate my birthday with, and he rocked celebrating my birthday. He picked me up at my house and handed me a rose. He walked me to his car and took me out to a local chain restaurant. Nothing fancy, but what he did made it the best night. We walked into the restaurant and the hostess recognized him and knew exactly where to take us. I walked around the corner and saw a giftbag and five other roses to match the one he had given me earlier.

He had gone to the restaurant ahead of time to have the gift and roses waiting at the table for me. It's one of the sweetest things anyone has ever done for me, even to this day. In the giftbag was a stuffed teddy bear. I kept it for years afterwards. I don't have it anymore, but I slept with it almost every night for years. Even though our relationship didn't last very long. He would always surprise me with sweet gifts like that.

I went to my locker one time, and inside was my favorite candy bar, a card, and a wrapped gift. The gift was a framed photo of the two of us. I was very confused why he had left the gift with me. It wasn't my birthday or anything like that. I ripped open the card, hoping it would help explain to me why I was getting this sweet gift. I learned it was our one-month anniversary. My thoughts: *It is?* And, *Crap! Is that a thing? Do couples celebrate one-month anniversaries?* I quickly took note of what day it was so I could do something for him for our two-month anniversary, which didn't really happen the way I had hoped it would.

He was my first make-out session, and the first and *only* guy to ever sneak over to my parents' house in the middle of the night. Why was he the only guy to do it? Because we got caught. Completely busted. My dad is just too good at knowing what high-school students do. My dog barked and woke my dad, who saw MyPrecious turn his car headlights off and park the car on the road of our secluded neighborhood. My dad was nervous and went out to legit look inside the freaking car. Of course, MyPrecious left his freaking wallet in the car (there wasn't much crime in my small town in Ohio). So, inside that wallet, my dad clearly saw MyPrecious' driver's license and knew whose car it was and that MyPrecious was definitely somewhere in the neighborhood—or in our house.

I was up in our attic with MyPrecious just talking about life. We were both going through teenage drama and just wanted to cuddle and talk through things. The most we did that night was make out. In fact, we never had sex with each other in high school. Not once. If we had, we certainly would not have done it in my parents' house while they were sleeping. Especially since MyPrecious' parents were always out of the house on business trips and we had it to ourselves a lot. (My parents never knew that). That is the complete truth, and it's what I've tried to tell my parents ever since. They still don't believe me.

MyPrecious was kicked out of my house that night, and I had a serious talk with them the next day. All about how I need to behave better and not lose my virginity. I assured them I was not having sex. They didn't believe me; they still don't believe me. In fact, after graduating college, I was riding in the car with my mom and she randomly told me, "I'm so happy you didn't get pregnant in high school." To which I responded, "Well, that would've been impossible since I didn't have sex in high school." She just smiled with that look of disbelief. Shrugs. What can you do?

Back to MyPrecious. We were boyfriend-and-girlfriend through the end of the year. He took me to prom, and it was a really fun night. He treated me like a princess. He kept a photo of us on his dashboard in his car, and we talked every day. Cellphones were just starting to grow in popularity, and when I started driving, my parents bought me my first very own cellphone, so I had my own line to call and text him from. Everything seemed to be going well. We had told each other "I love you." I remember him saying it to me first. I thought it was a bit soon, but I felt the same way (or my high-school self thought that's what I was feeling), so I said it back.

Years later, he told me that I had misheard him. He tended to talk fast and mumble. He didn't want to embarrass me by correcting me, so he just went with it. Awkward. My first "I love you" wasn't even a true "I love you." And that is real life, folks.

Everything seemed to be going well. We were happy. Then summer came. I had been accepted to be a Junior Counselor at a summer camp I had attended for years in North Carolina. The camp is a three-week program during which you have no access to technology. The only way for us to talk with each other was to write letters. I received two letters from him during camp and wrote him back. In the letters, he would tell me how he missed me and loved me (or so I thought before he told me later about the mistake). The three weeks seemed to go by fast for me. I had a great time, but I couldn't wait to get back home and see MyPrecious.

Once I got home, I went over to see him. I tried to sit on his lap and give him a kiss, but he was standoffish. It wasn't the same anymore. He didn't seem interested in me. *Crap*. My plan had backfired. My plan to not be the one to get hurt. To be able to break things off and come out unscathed. It didn't work. I asked him what was going on. He was honest with me. More than I can say about most of the other guys

I've dated since him. He told me he had developed feelings for another girl. She was a grade younger than us. Oh, and she was also one of my good friends who I danced and cheered with. I was going to be seeing a lot of her. Ouch.

I cried. I cried a lot. I tried to hang out with him again. I couldn't just hang out with him. I still had feelings for him, and it was obvious that he was no longer interested in me. We would go to the movies together by ourselves. Thinking about it now, that's much more of a date than a friend hangout, but I guess there really wasn't too much to do in my small town. I would fight the urge to look at him or hold his hand the entire movie. Yeah. This was definitely not going to work. I couldn't suppress those feelings every time we hung out, and I wasn't going to move on if we kept hanging out.

Now, what some people do during situations like this is blame the girl their ex likes. They get upset with her and are hateful towards her. Why? Clearly it's jealousy. It makes no sense. I was never angry with this new girl. She was my friend and had done nothing to me. I was gone and he had developed feelings for her. It was as simple as that. She is still a friend of mine to this day. So listen up, people. Stop being mean or rude or hateful towards the other person that your ex likes if they haven't done anything but gain your ex's attraction. (Unless, of course, they cheated and caused the breakup—then I get it!). You should be upset with your ex. Well, actually, you just have to move on and find someone that wants to be with you. Forget them both!

So that was the end of my first real relationship—my first relationship in which we exchanged *I-love-you*s to each other. In fact, it is the only relationship in which I've exchanged *I-love-you*s (even though they ended up not even being real *I-love-yous*).

Don't get me wrong. It's not as easy as just snapping your fingers to get over a person. It takes time. It takes a lot of distractions. It takes friends willing to listen to you talk about your ex and how much you still care about them and want to date them. I definitely talked about him. I talked about him *a lot*. I wanted him to want me back, but I wanted him to want me back on his own terms. So, when I wasn't thinking about how much I missed our relationship or how much I missed him, I dove head first into distractions.

I finished up my summer with soccer practice and dance practice. I jumped back into focusing on college and trying to get over MyPrecious and move on. It was hard. I was crushed. But life does move on.

I didn't date anyone my senior-year of high school, but man, did I enjoy it! One of my favorite quotes in life is , "Live Well. It is the greatest revenge," from The Talmud.

Every time someone hurts me, I try and do something else that betters my life or someone else's life. I volunteer, or go on a run or go on a fun trip. It feels amazing. My senior year was just that. I was our Homecoming Queen, I won a local pageant, and I was accepted into the college I wanted—Loyola University Chicago.

The.NextDoor.Neighbor

I was single, but I was rocking it and having the time of my life. The countdown to college and my goal of leaving my small town was getting lower and lower. While I was focused on finishing up high school on a high note, a guy was focused on finding a way to meet me. He lived in my neighborhood but was older than me. He was already in college at a school in Ohio and had been home on Christmas break. He had seen me walking in the neighborhood and wanted to meet me. He was TheNextDoorNeighbor. I'm sure a lot of people have had those relationships in their lives. In fact, most people in the past didn't have the internet to meet new people. They met people who lived within a block of their homes.

TheNextDoorNeighbor didn't just have his parents introduce us or walk to our house and say hello. He probably would've come across a little weird to me if he had. Instead, he knew a guy who went to the same high school as me. He asked that friend to tell me he was interested in meeting me. One day, you're walking down the hall to class like every other day and minding your own business, and a guy walks up to you to tell you some guy wants to meet you. I told him, "Sure." To just let me know when he wanted to meet me.

I mean, why not? I was pretty sure I had seen him in our neighborhood and he looked good, if he was the guy I thought I saw. He was older, too. That's what I needed—an older man. A couple weeks went by, and then I got a text message from the guy at school asking if I wanted to go over to TheNextDoorNeighbor's house to meet him. I had one of my best friends over and decided I could definitely do it, especially with my wing-woman by my side.

I texted back, *Sure, my friend and I will walk over now.* Little did I know, this would be the beginning of a long, confusing relationship.

We knocked on the door, and TheNextDoorNeighbor answered and introduced himself. I was so nervous. My heart was racing. He was really attractive. Much more attractive than the other guys in my high school. He was really nice, too. He was friendly to both me and my friend. We hung out that night for a little bit and exchanged numbers. I knew we would see each other, again. How could we not? We lived less than a quarter-mile away from each other, and clearly we were attracted to each other.

TheNextDoorNeighbor returned to college shortly after we met. I would have to wait until the summer to find out what would happen between us. I went back to finishing up high school, this time with no distractions. I no longer cared about the high-school guys. I wanted to see what would happen with TheNextDoorNeighbor. I couldn't wait for summer to come.

Summer came quickly. I lived in a neighborhood where several houses shared a large lake. We had a boat, canoe, and kayak that we could use to paddle around on the hot summer days. TheNextDoorNeighbor and I both had summer jobs in the city and would spend our nights and weekends together paddling or swimming in the lake. He taught me how to fish and drove me around on the country roads that surrounded our small city, the wind blowing my hair all over my face as I laughed. It was one of those summers you see in the movies or hear about in songs. We would explore abandoned barns and hike around in the dark woods. We were carefree and enjoying life without a thought of putting a title on things, or trying to find out where our relationship would go. I think we both knew on some level that our "thing" was just something for the summer. Whatever our "thing" was, it was awesome. We held hands and kissed. We went to the drive-in theater and cuddled. We just enjoyed each other's company.

MyPrecious

All I could think about that summer was TheNextDoorNeighbor. MyPrecious was no longer a thought in my mind. And that's when it happens. Once you forget about them, that's when they come back. MyPrecious did just that. He was the first guy from my past to do this. He wouldn't be the last. Almost all of them always come back.

He called me. It was one night in the summer when I had just pulled into the garage with my parents. He called to talk to me and admit to me that he wished he could change how things ended between us. How he regretted breaking up with me. (No, he wasn't drunk.) My eyes got wider and wider the more he said. I was in disbelief. He said all the words I always wanted to hear from him. The words I had dreamed of hearing just a few weeks ago. Now, they were just words.

I didn't know how to respond. I was happy he finally realized my worth, but I had moved on and put him in my past. I awkwardly laughed and told him, "You mean, like that song by Cher?" I then sang (off key), "If I could turn back time…" We both laughed, and he said, "Yes, Ashley, something like that." We talked a little more that night, but I wasn't going to return to my feelings for him so quickly. He broke my heart, and I was guarded. Plus, I had way too much fun with TheNextDoorNeighbor to want to go back to him.

I wish I could say I never let him back in, but as I said earlier, I like to learn lessons the hard way. I didn't let him back in that night, though. I thanked him for his kind words and wished him luck in college.

I went back to my summer adventures with TheNextDoorNeighbor, and before I knew it, the summer was over. I was saying goodbye to him and my town. We both said our goodbyes, content knowing we would always remember our summer together. Knowing there were probably going to be many more summers to look forward to making more memories. But also knowing it was time to go our separate ways, and it was time to let each other go for now.

I packed up my parents' minivan, and we pulled out of our driveway to head to Chicago. I said my silent goodbyes to high school, to MyPrecious, to my summer of fun with TheNextDoorNeighbor. It was truly a *good*bye. I enjoyed every minute of that high-school rollercoaster ride.

As my parents drove the four-and a half hours to Chicago from our hometown, I continued to wear a smile that would remain for the next four years. I was going to college, and I was going to college single. *Chicago—here I come! High school—see ya later*. Another chapter of my dating life had ended. It gave me a lot of good life lessons, but I was sure it was going to be much better in college.

3 | College
(The M.R.S. Degree)

There it was: the Chicago skyline stretching across the windshield of our van. I had finally made it to my future. We drove down Lakeshore Drive and there was little I could do to control the excitement bubbling up inside me. I was going to the school of my dreams and living in the city of my dreams. The city seemed limitless to me, with an unlimited number of opportunities, an unlimited number of possibilities. An unlimited number of men to meet. Most importantly, with *freedom*.

My parents helped unload my stuff from the car into my new dorm room. (Mertz 'til it hurts!) Then they took me out to dinner and wanted to take me out to do more things. As much as I was going to miss my family, I wanted my freedom more. I was ready to live on my own—well, live with a bunch of other people my age and do whatever I wanted. I wanted to explore and break the rules. I thanked my parents for everything and said my goodbyes. My parents seemed a little sad to leave me, but all I was thinking was that I would see them for Thanksgiving. (I think they did a really good job teaching me how to be independent.) As soon as they drove away, I ran back upstairs to my dorm room where my roommate was waiting. I wasn't going to waste any time. I was going to start exploring and breaking rules that first night on campus.

Mr. FirstNightOfCollege

My freshman-year roommate is still a friend today. She had more freedom growing up than I did. I didn't need much help jumping outside my comfort zone, but the little help I did need she gave to me. We decided that night we needed to start the college life off right. We needed to meet boys and drink some alcohol. The only problem was we didn't have any alcohol and we didn't know any guys. So we decided we'd go and meet guys that had alcohol for us. Two birds, one stone.

How does one find guys and alcohol in a dorm room? Easy. Step one: sneak up to the guys' floor (every other floor was a guys' floor). Step two: listen for loud party music. Step three: knock on the door and ask if they have any alcohol to share. It took us about five minutes to find a room. College life is awesome. There were two guys, and they were playing music by Mike Jones. Why do I remember that? The song they were playing had Mike Jones saying his name over and over again. They had that song on repeat. All night. I will never listen to that song again.

They invited us in and had filtered a bottle of cheap vodka through a water filter pitcher. So clever. They claimed the filtering made the liquor better and gave you less of a hangover. We believed them. (My hangover the next day did not). The two guys were nice and flirted with us both. One spent more time with my roommate. The other, we'll call him Mr. FirstNightOfCollege, hung out with me. We both kissed the guys that night. First college kiss with a stranger. None of us in that room expected anything more that night. Nothing more happened between us that night. We didn't hang out with those guys again, just exchanged a friendly hello if we happened to pass by each other on campus. It was the start of many similar interactions with other guys. I was just trying to figure out what I wanted and what I liked.

Mr. TooMuchTooSoon

My first college crush happened pretty quickly. Another tall, quiet blonde. His looks were not what made me like him, though. (I mean, it helped that he was hot). I liked him because he was a really sweet guy and athletic, but he was really shy. He was a great guy. He played ultimate frisbee on campus and used to go to an all-guys school in Missouri. We started off as friends and I started to flirt with him more and more. For whatever reason, I had chosen him as the guy I wanted to date first at Loyola.

We hung out together a lot to watch movies or grab lunch in the cafeteria. He was everything I should have wanted in a guy, but it was all starting to be too much for me. He was Mr. TooMuchTooSoon.

I was in a new city, at a new school, and meeting so many new people every single day. I liked hanging out with Mr. TooMuchTooSoon, but I also couldn't let go of the possibility of meeting someone else.

The start of college was a short transition from high school. Since it was such a short transition, I still didn't know what I was doing relationship-wise. I had no idea how things were supposed to work or how couples started dating. (Let's be honest, I still don't.) So Mr. TooMuchTooSoon and I just kept hanging out a lot. Enjoying our time together. I was taking things slow and not looking to the future. I wasn't ready to commit to him, or really to anybody. I still thought about MyPrecious and I was hurt by how it had all ended. I was protecting myself and enjoying my freedom.

Mr. TooMuchTooSoon had other plans, though. He was ready to define our relationship. He was also already proudly telling all of his friends how amazing he thought our relationship would be. He didn't tell me these things; I would find out, though. When I did find out, I ran. I ran towards singlehood as quickly as I could. Facebook was the catalyst for this full-on sprint away from boyfriend/girlfriend status.

Facebook was created just a couple years before I started at Loyola. When it first started, anyone that signed up was required to have a college email address. It was an exciting new exclusive social platform to share my college experiences without my parents having access (until, you know, everyone and their mom got access and now my grandma can see my Facebook page). Back then, I was young and I was dumb.

Although Facebook has changed a lot through the years, it still had a "relationship status" option back then. You could notify everyone on your friends list if you were single, in an open relationship, or dating someone. If you were in a relationship with someone, you could tag them to your relationship status so all of your friends could click on the person's name and stalk your new lover. Nowadays, once you change your status, a notification is sent to all of your friends and they can comment or "like" it. Luckily, all you could do back then was like a post. Now, people can actually select a laughing or a surprised face when you notify them about your relationship status. Facebook was a great way to stay connected and invite others to college parties, but it was also one more way for all of your peers to judge you. Not just your college peers, but all those high school peers that I tried so hard to leave in my past.

It was also a new, harsh, impersonal way for couples to broadcast dating and break ups. Although you could tag a person in your Facebook relationship status, the other person had to accept your tag. Now guys had a way to ask a girl to be in a relationship with them without even talking to them face-to-face. I also had friends who learned of their breakups because the guy changed his status and no longer had her tagged. Ouch. This is just the beginning of how the internet would change dating—sometimes for the better, sometimes for the worse.

Mr. TooMuchTooSoon was not one of those guys that used Facebook to ask me to be his girlfriend. He was more respectful, or the tool was just so new to us that he didn't even think about it. Instead, he brought me up to his room and asked me, "Ashley, would you go out with me?" I think a better question would be to ask me to be his girlfriend. But back then, "going out" was synonymous with asking someone to be your boyfriend or girlfriend.

I was nervous and a bit scared when he started to ask the question. I knew it was coming; it was inevitable. We had hung out a lot and he wanted to define our hangouts. I forced a smile. That's right, forced it. I said yes in a fake-cheerful manner and told him I had to go study. I gave him a quick hug and ran out of his room. I ran to the elevator and pushed the button over and over again until it came to rescue me from his floor. I entered the elevator and was overcome with regret. Not the best feeling to have when you start a new relationship.

By the time I got to my dorm room and opened my computer, Mr. TooMuchTooSoon already sent me a request to be in a Facebook relationship with me.

Ugh. Again, not the response I should have had if I really liked him. I grudgingly accepted the request. I forgot in that instant what would happen next. I was quickly reminded by tons of likes and comments from people who went to my high school. Comments from people I wanted to keep in my past. Comments from people who barely talked to me in high school. Comments congratulating me and asking me about this guy. I did not like this. I did not like any of this. Not only was I not sure about the relationship, now I was having to deal with all these questions from people I didn't want questions from.

Then I got a friend request and message from this guy. He was a good friend of Mr. TooMuchTooSoon. Men and women, tell your friends now to never do this for you. Never do this when your friend just made a relationship official. This good friend of Mr. TooMuchTooSoon sent me what could have been an amazing message if he had better timing. I would of enjoyed the message if I had been in a long-term, serious, close-to-engagement relationship with Mr. TooMuchTooSoon. I wasn't, though. I was in a short-term (maybe a month) uncertain relationship.

I had never met this friend. In fact, I don't remember Mr. TooMuchTooSoon even talking to me about this friend. The friend sent me a message telling me how amazing I am and how lucky Mr. TooMuchTooSoon was to have found a girl like me. The more I read, the more I felt like Mr. TooMuchTooSoon told this friend that we were going to get married. The more I read, the more I couldn't breathe, and the more I questioned this relationship. I was certainly not on the same page. I was barely eighteen years old, and I was nowhere near wanting to settle down and get married. I didn't even know what I wanted to study in college. I panicked. I closed out of Facebook like that would make it all disappear. All of it was way too much for me, and it was all way too soon.

I took some time for myself and kept my distance a little from Mr. TooMuchTooSoon, but still gave him a chance. He invited me to Loyola's President's Ball, and that was when I finalized my decision on our relationship. (The President's Ball is similar to a homecoming dance, but they hand out awards. We went because it was the freshman thing to do).

He was sweet to me all night and treated me like a boyfriend should. I, however, was annoyed by him following me around the dance. I was annoyed that he was treating me like his girlfriend. It was then I knew I had to end things with him. I just wasn't ready to be in a relationship, and I definitely didn't share the same feelings for him that he had for me. I told him that night that I no longer wanted to be in a relationship with him. He is still the only guy where I was the one to end our relationship.

I didn't want to hurt him and felt bad that he seemed hurt that I didn't want to date him. But I never regretted that decision. Even today. He's married now to a beautiful woman he met right after me at Loyola. I'm happy for him, and I finally was happy with myself. I was back to being single in the city I loved. I was back to being content and happy. I was back to freedom and finding myself.

MyPrecious

Shortly after the formal, before we left for the holidays, a guy from my past came back to haunt me via text message:

Hey Ash! I'm going to be in Chicago to see my sister next weekend. Can we meet up?

It was MyPrecious. He was back. Again.

My head immediately filled with a million thoughts. *What do I do? Should I see him? Why does he want to see me? Should I ignore this? What does he want?*

I decided to take some time and think about it. I eventually decided to text him back and agreed to meet up with him. What was the worst that could happen? It had been months since I thought about him or had any feelings for him. I thought maybe we could finally be friends.

The next weekend, I met him at his sister's apartment and went with them to get dinner. We laughed and had a great time. *Oh, crap.* I still had feelings for him. They were still there and I had just pushed them down. They were slowly creeping up as dinner progressed. I figured, *It's just one night. I can handle one night. Then he'll go back to Ohio and I can push those feelings right back down.*

We ended dinner, and he decided to come back to Loyola with me to go out to a party. We went out and he met all of my friends. I was introducing him proudly. I was introducing him as if maybe we could get back together. What. Was. I. Thinking? Maybe I'd had too much to drink. I'll blame it on that.

I slowly started flirting more with him and touching him more. He wasn't feeling it. He kept pushing my hands off him. You'd think I'd take the hint. I didn't. I tried to kiss him and he did not reciprocate. Ouch. He had gotten over his feelings for me. I had lowered my guard for him again. He'd punched my heart again. I didn't talk to him for a month after that night. He tried to reach out to me and talk to me. I didn't want to talk to him. He had fooled me. Not once, but twice. It was my fault that he fooled me this time. I wasn't going to let him fool me again. But not just him; I wasn't going to let any guy fool me again. (Or so I thought.)

I finished up the rest of the semester wearing sweatpants to class every day. I was no longer dressing to impress any guy. I was over them. I went home for winter break that year and just spent time with my family. Family is always a good distraction.

Sometimes you just need a weekend away from life and back with your family. Then you start to realize that things will be okay.

I went back to spring semester refreshed with an almost fully-patched heart. I went back with a Miss Independent attitude. I was going to do spring semester for me. Screw guys. They suck. (Except as friends; guy friends are totally okay).

Mr. Italiano

I started second semester like I'd finished first: in sweats. I no longer cared what new guys were in my class or what I looked like. All I wanted to do was get through class and hang out with my friends. That's what I wanted. Mr. Italiano had different plans.

Mr. Italiano was in my philosophy 101 class, one of those core classes everyone is required to take in college. It was a small class of about twenty-five people. We sat in a semicircle. He was across the room from me. He was tall, fit, dark-haired with beautiful big eyes. The typical handsome Italian-American (think John Tucker from the movie *John Tucker Must Die*) man from a fairytale. You couldn't miss him.

I started daydreaming about this prince, maybe changing my mind about guys. Maybe this was the guy that I've been waiting to meet. This was the guy that would sweep me off my feet and care for me. As quickly as those thoughts started to enter my mind, my inner voice yelled at me. *Snap out of it, Ashley! This is you-time. You're not pursuing another guy. You're done. You're being single and enjoying it!* I was in the middle of talking myself out of it when Mr. Italiano gave my inner voice a little support.

He just opened his mouth. (How quickly someone can gain or lose attractiveness when they start talking.) He lost attractiveness. He was one of those know-it-alls, a teacher's pet. As soon as the professor asked a question, he shot his hand into the air with a smirk on his face. The excitement shooting out of him was freaking annoying.

Uggggghhhhhh, I thought. He was one of THOSE people. Don't get me wrong. I love a man who's smart. I love a man who reads and wants to learn new things. I don't love a man who shoves the fact that he's smart down everyone's throat. He was raising his hand to prove to all of us in class that he knew the answer. To prove to the teacher that he was the smartest in the class and he was getting an A this semester. Barf.

He was one of those people you just wanted to prove wrong. You wanted to argue the opposite of what they argue to get under their skin. You also wanted to thank them just a little bit, because as annoying as these people are, they also tend to make class move along without you having to participate. So, as much as I was starting to despise him more and more, I also appreciated the fact the teacher looked to fewer people to answer questions. You know, since he knew them all.

During that first class, he kept looking at me. He wouldn't stop looking my way. I looked back at him and thought, *What the hell? Is there something on my face?*, with a look on my face to match my inner thoughts. I never was good at hiding my emotions.

I was wearing sweats, for crying out loud. My hair was the same as how I slept in it the night before. My makeup was pretty much non-existent. I had no idea why this guy would continue to beg for my attention. I was annoyed, but also intrigued. I'll admit he left an impression on me. I won't say it was a completely positive impression, but it was an impression.

I didn't want him to be on my mind when I left the class, but I couldn't stop thinking about him. The whole interaction. It was so weird.

I brushed it off, though. I didn't want to date anyone (I kept telling myself). I certainly wasn't looking for a boyfriend. I didn't trust any guy, and I wasn't going to trust him. He was arrogant. He was one of those guys that always ended up hurting the girl in the end. I wasn't going to let it happen this time. He wasn't going to win my attention. I wasn't going to allow him to hurt me.

As classes continued, we all learned each other's names. Mr. Italiano apparently made it his job to memorize my name first. Not only did he memorize it, he continued to use it in class.

I would spend a lot of the class day-dreaming. He would spend most of class answering all of the questions, which allowed me to zone out. Until he started to include me in his answers.

"Don't you agree, Ashley?" I would snap out of my daydream at the sound of my name. In my head I was thinking, *Um, I was just daydreaming about doing a roundoff back tuck across this floor. I have no idea what you just said. So, I have no idea whether I agree with you. You freaking jerk.* On the outside, I saw the whole class now looking at me. I just shrugged my shoulders and said, "Yup. What you said."

I would then stare at him with a look of confusion and annoyance. Who was this guy? What was his problem? Couldn't he see that I wasn't interested in interacting with him? Doesn't he see the "Screw All Men" shining brightly across my forehead? I just rolled my eyes and went back to my daydream.

His desire to get my attention didn't end there. It continued throughout the semester to the point where my friend told me, "You know he likes you, right?" I told her, "No he doesn't." She rolled her eyes and said, "Yeah he does. It's the freaking *Ashley and Mr. Italiano* show every class." I just shrugged my shoulders.

So what if he liked me? He seemed like one of those guys who thought he could get any girl he wanted. One of those guys who crossed the line from confident to cocky. He didn't just cross it, he jumped across that line. He was the guy who would lead a girl on just for the game. He wanted the chase, but not the relationship. I didn't want the relationship from him either. So I figured, *What the hell*. I'd play his game.

I played along with his antics, but only giving him enough to want to flirt just a little more. I never dressed up for him or asked for his attention. I just responded and maybe gave him a little smile or side comment. Then I'd leave class and go about my day. Unfortunately, I'm more of a short-term game player. I lose when I go for the long game. I lose every time.

Mr. Italiano started bringing his class antics outside of class. He ran out after me one day to ask what I was doing later that night. I told him I didn't have any plans. He said we should meet up either that night or sometime. I shrugged my shoulders and said, "Sure." I was going to make him set the plans, though. He never did. I didn't think he would.

Then I started running into him in our common areas. He would make a point to talk to me. I finally worked up the courage to ask him to join my friend and me for a comedy event in the basement of one of the dorms. I didn't think he would show. To my surprise, he did. He came with his friend and we all hungout and laughed until he excused himself to go back to the library. He took his studies really seriously.

Soon I met his close friends. There were three of them. Three guys who all studied something in the sciences. All of them took their studies seriously. I usually ran into them at the library. I finally started to go to the library more that second semester. I was hoping to run into Mr. Italiano, but I also really needed to get more serious about school. I was on a scholarship and needed to maintain a minimum GPA to keep it. Keep my grades up and potentially run into a guy? The library is where it's at.

Unfortunately (but later I would consider it fortunate), I only ran into Mr. Italiano's friends at the library and not Mr. Italiano. He hid out in the stacks and his friends were always in the common area at one of the shared tables. They were always nice and always asked me to join their tables. I became better and better friends with them and they taught me how to have better study habits. Thanks to them, I kept my scholarship. But also thanks to them, I got into my first fight with Mr. Italiano.

I was leaving the library during finals week. Loyola had events during the week that helped us get through the stressful time. One event was a free waffle night in a nearby dining hall. One of Mr. Italiano's friends had been studying with me in the library and we both decided to take a break and go get some. I mean, it's free waffles. Who would say no to free waffles?

As we were leaving the library, Mr. Italiano ran into us. We asked him if he wanted to join us on our free waffle trip. He got mad. Really mad. I got confused. Really confused.

He started screaming at both of us. I'm not exaggerating, either. He was full-fledged screaming and losing it. He was mad at his friend because his friend was supposed to go with him to get waffles, and instead, his friend was walking with me to get them. We kept explaining that we hadn't made plans and we just decided to go. We told him he was invited. He didn't listen. He told me I was trying to take his friends from him. It was crazy.

He didn't talk to me the rest of the semester, and it hurt. His friend told me not to worry about it. He told me Mr. Italiano has a bad temper and he'll get over it. I left school to return home for the summer. I was really confused about what happened with Mr. Italiano. I hadn't even dated the guy and it went south really fast.

I sent him a Facebook message apologizing for anything I did that hurt him and telling him I hoped we could still be friends. I figured if I couldn't date him then I would at least try to be friends with him. I had enjoyed hanging out with him and I really didn't want to lose his friendship or the friendship I had developed with his friends. Plus, I had a feeling I would be seeing a lot more of them during my time at Loyola. So, we might as well be friendly.

He didn't answer me, at least not right away. I left that summer thinking I probably wouldn't hear from Mr. Italiano, again. But, like I said before, they always come back.

TheHighSchoolGuyAtARandomCollegeParty

I returned back to my summer job with the city after my freshman year. I was one of the first back to my hometown after school. Loyola was on semesters, and Ohio State, where most of my high-school friends went for college, was on quarters at the time. They were all still in school. My best friend from high school was there and invited me and a few of my other friends to come down for a toga party. *Toga! Toga! Toga!*

I picked up my other friend and we drove down to Ohio State, full of excitement for the weekend. I was eager to find out what it was like to party at a different school.

We found parking and grabbed our bags to head up to our friend's dorm room. We walked into a tiny room shared by four girls. We were going to crash on the floor, but really we spent most of the night out.

We all crowded into the small dorm bathroom and got ready for the night. I wore a pillowcase as my toga outfit. Oh, college.

Most of us were single and still trying to figure ourselves out. We walked around campus until we found my friend's friend's toga party. That's how it worked. You'd go to a party where your friends knew someone related to the party. You would meet all new people. Plenty of single people. If only adult life had those options. Now you have to traverse the party trying not to be obvious as you look for wedding rings and arms around others—members of couples marking their territory.

I met a lot of different people that night, but even when you meet a lot of different people, you tend to go back to what's familiar to you. I did the same that night. A guy from my high school went to Ohio State and I still had his number in my phone. We never dated during school, but we flirted heavily. Now was our chance to see what would happen.

We flirtatiously texted each other all night, trying to find a way to meet up. Ohio State's campus is huge. We didn't end up meeting up until later that night. We had a couple drinks with each other and headed back to my friend's dorm room. We kissed that night. It wasn't anything special. It was actually pretty awkward. But we finally crossed the line from friends into maybe something more.

We at least tried to see what it would be like. It wasn't all that great. It was definitely a one-time kind of thing. He was just going to be

TheHighSchoolGuyAtA-RandomCollegeParty.   For some, this would be a start to something much more, a long-term relationship or even a marriage. For me, it was a single awkward night. There would be more conversations in the future, but nothing more.

TheNextDoorNeighbor

I drove back home, thankful for the fun weekend with friends. I was also excited to get back home and await the arrival of TheNextDoorNeighbor. I was looking forward to another summer of swimming in the lake and driving on those country roads without a care in the world.

It's funny how you can be such good friends with a guy and he still doesn't tell you everything about their life. How they tell everyone you're the best of friends, and they text you, call you, and spend as much time as possible with you, but they still hold back. They say you're friends, but the conversation of relationships and dating never comes up. You don't talk about the dates you go on with other people. You don't talk about those other people at all. They just don't seem important, until one day they become important.

Now, it's awkward. You're dating someone, but you never told your best of friends about them. You didn't tell them about the dates. You barely even mentioned his or her name. It's almost as if you cheated on your friend, but you were never in a relationship. That's how I learned about TheNextDoorNeighbor's new girlfriend.

He came back home for the summer, this time with a serious girlfriend. This summer wasn't going to be the same as last summer. I would have to be careful, and we would spend less time together. I was happy for him, but also confused that he hadn't told me about her. Why had he been so silent about her during our conversations over the year?

I told him I was happy for him and put my wall up and kept my distance. I wanted to be his friend, but when we were together, we didn't act like friends. We acted like teenage crushes. I refocused myself on my work and getting back to college as quickly as possible. As fun as our summer adventures had been, we weren't going to start them back up this year. We were officially just friends, and he had a serious girlfriend.

I wasn't really upset, though. Sure, I was going to miss enjoying those moments again with him. But we were never serious and we also knew that it would be over when the summer ended. It just ended before the summer got started this time. It was time for me to move on, too.

Mr. Italiano

As the summer drew to a close, I went over to a high-school friend's house for an end-of-the-summer party. I was hanging out in his basement and catching up with old friends (and old flings—MyPrecious). We were all just hanging out and having a good time. I was excited to see everyone, but I was more excited to head back to Loyola. I didn't have cellphone reception in the basement. I had one of those early model flip phones, and cell service was just starting to work out its issues.

I went back upstairs to finish up my goodbyes and head home. I checked my phone and saw I had a missed voicemail. Back then, phones didn't tell you who the missed message was from, or at least my phone didn't. I got nervous thinking it was my parents and they wanted to know when I was coming home. No matter how old you get or how much freedom you have in college or living as an adult, when you come back home, the rules are always the same. You've got to check in with your parents and not stay out too late.

I quickly hit the button to listen to the voicemail. A little annoyed that my parents were calling when it wasn't even that late, yet. Then I heard a familiar voice. It wasn't my mom or dad. It was Mr. Italiano. I didn't even know what he said the first time I listened to it. I was in shock that I was hearing his voice on the other line. *What? He'd called me? He actually wants to talk to me?*

They always come back.

My mouth dropped open and my eyes grew wide as the voicemail finished. Everyone around me wanted to know what was wrong. I explained to them that I had met a guy in school, but I was confident he was never going to talk to me again. I was apparently wrong. He had called me. He called me!!!

I replayed the voicemail and actually listened to the words this time. He still wanted to be friends. He was excited for school to start back up and to see me. A smile spread across my face and butterflies filled my stomach. I know I said I just wanted to be his friend, but there was something about him. I couldn't wait to get back to school and see him and spend more time with him. He was one of those guys who caught my eye and made me wonder if he could be the one for me. I was hoping to find out.

The end of summer flew by after that night. I talked with Mr. Italiano a little here and there and couldn't wait to get back to Chicago. Before I knew it, I was in my parents' minivan driving that four and a half hour drive back to my favorite city. Back to another year of college. Back to another year of freedom and finding out a little more about Mr. Italiano.

Sophomore year I moved in with a friend I met my freshman year. We got to be really good friends over the summer and she started off being a great wing-woman. The weekend after we moved in, Mr. Italiano invited me over to a birthday party for one of the three guys in his friends' group. I asked my roommate to come along with me.

We danced all night and had a great time. Mr. Italiano and I flirted most of the night, and I was excited to see where things would go with him. We picked up right where we had left off. He continued to try and get my attention at the party and I played along. We took a couple of cute photos and then we said our goodbyes and headed to bed for the night. Most of the rest of our flirting that first semester of sophomore year was on instant messenger. How confident men can be when they're not talking to you in person and hiding behind the screen of a computer.

He would ask me to hangout every once in a while, but it was always in groups or it was an awkward handful of minutes in my dorm room as I was doing laundry. He never asked to take me on a date or go out. His games were starting to get annoying. Again, he never mentioned any other girls to me. He never talked about seeing other girls or other girls wanting to be with him. He never told me about them until the last minute, or his friends told me about them.

His friends would tell me how he had a lot of girls after him. How the girls threw themselves at him and drove by his place to see him. *What? That's crazy. Those girls are crazy*. But you know what? It worked. They usually got him. At least for a little bit.

No, thanks, I thought. I wasn't going to be one of those girls. If he wanted to date me, then he was going to have to put forth the effort. I wasn't going to pursue him. Instead, I focused back on my mantra: to live well. I wanted a new adventure. I wanted something that pushed me out of my boundaries and distracted me from Mr. Italiano for a while. I wanted to study abroad.

Maybe I was running away from my problems. Running away is usually my first response to danger. Whatever you want to call it, I'm glad I did.

I went to Loyola's administration office to find out what my options were for a study-abroad location. I wanted to go somewhere completely different than the United States. Somewhere most people never traveled or lived if they were born in the United States. I had met a camp instructor a few summers earlier who taught African drum and dance. He was from Ghana. I decided to look and see if there were any programs there. Lucky me, there was a program, and I was still within the deadline to apply.

I quickly completed the application and found out I could go abroad that second semester of my sophomore year. I poured myself into the application process and received approval. Then I worked on getting all of my shots up to date and a passport. I was going to study in Ghana. I was going to live somewhere new and have a new adventure for an entire semester. I couldn't wait.

Mr. Italiano was not happy with me. He didn't understand why I wanted to travel to Ghana at all. I didn't care. I was doing the trip for me and not for him. Mr. Italiano wanted me to stay and didn't want me to go. Again, I didn't care. I thought if we were meant to be together, then it would work out. I continued to finalize the study-abroad program.

Mr. TheFeelingWasn'tThere

I focused my attention on finishing up my classes for the semester and making sure I had everything lined up for my study-abroad program. I no longer cared what would happen between Mr. Italiano and me. I went out with my friends and had fun. I tried to enjoy the rest of my time at Loyola that semester. As I was leaving my dorm room one night to go out and meet my friends, I ran into Mr. TheFeelingWasn'tThere. He was really outgoing and stopped me as I was walking away from my dorm room.

He asked me where I was going, and I told him I was meeting up with friends. We talked a little back and forth. Then he asked me, "Where have you been hiding all my life?" To which I answered directly, "Um, I live right there," and pointed to the dorm building behind him. We both laughed and told each other to have a good night. I wasn't crazy about him, but there was something about him that intrigued me. We went our separate ways that night, but we ended up bumping into each other a few times on campus, and he added me as a friend on Facebook. He was nice and sweet. But I was moving to Ghana next semester. So, nothing was going to happen. Nothing ever did end up happening either. He continued to pursue me throughout the rest of college, but there was a little voice inside me telling me we weren't the right fit. I didn't understand it at the time, and I wanted so badly to like him.

He wrote me poems that I've kept to this day. Describing my hair as golden locks from the sun and how he thought I was beautiful and amazing. *What is wrong with me? Why didn't I like this guy? He's saying all the right things and genuinely cares about me!* Still, no matter what he said or did, I just didn't want to date him.

Years later, he finally came out to the world. He has since found someone new to share is life with and I'm very happy for him. It was one more guy who taught me to always trust my gut. I truly believe you need to have a connection with someone if you want to date them. If you feel like you're missing that connection, trust your instincts and let each other go. It's the only way you can both find someone you're actually meant to share your life with.

Mr. Italiano

I had grown close to Mr. Italiano and his friends again. No matter how close we got, I wasn't going to change my mind about traveling and living in Ghana for the second semester of my sophomore year. (I'm pretty stubborn.) I'll admit, their send-off for me was really sweet and had me questioning my decision for a hot second. Then one of my life beliefs quickly confirmed my decision.

One of my life beliefs is if a person is your true friend or meant to be in your life, they will always be there no matter what path you take in life. They will always be your friend despite distance. I felt the same about Mr. Italiano and his friends. I also felt like he needed some space from me. He needed to see what it felt like without me there. I thought he'd realize he was missing out on having an amazing woman in his life. I think he started to realize it even before I left.

We all gathered in a restaurant along the Chicago River to laugh about recent memories and for me to say goodbye to them all until I returned for the summer. Later that night, I was told Mr. Italiano found a song and printed out all of the lyrics. He tried to get his friends to learn the song on the train ride to the restaurant to sing to me. (*How sweet is that?*)

The song was a backstreet boys' song called "Never Gone." It was a song about how no matter how far two people are, they will always be in each other's hearts. If there was a sign for a guy to show me that he liked me, I thought for sure this would most definitely be one. I mean, just put the book down right now. Go out to YouTube and listen to this song! Listen! Read the lyrics! (But as I'll learn, don't assume a guy likes you. Don't think anything until he actually *tells* you how he feels.)

He never did get a chance to sing the song to me that night, but I downloaded the song and played it a lot when I was overseas. Any time I was homesick, I would play it and it would calm me down. He never told me he would miss me, but I could tell. He was still asking me to stay even that night. He would learn that when I make up my mind, I follow through. I would miss him, though.

We all said our goodbyes, and I left for a four-month hiatus from my United States dating life and traveled to learn new things about another country—and about myself.

Mr. Norwegian

Africa is hot. Specifically, Accra, Ghana, Africa is freaking hot. I arrived in this foreign country as a minority. Only one-percent of people living in the country were white, and of those one percent, even fewer were blonde women. I stood out like a sore thumb. I was beginning to *slightly* understand what it felt like to be a minority in my hometown.

I spent the first month in the country trying to figure out how to safely live and eat. I took a pill every night and slept under a bug net to prevent getting sick from Malaria. I walked about forty-five minutes to class every day and mostly ate fried egg and vegetable sandwiches for every meal. I learned to appreciate the wide range of restaurants and convenience of transportation in America.

On the University of Ghana's campus, I was very different than most women. I was easy to spot out in a crowd and men there didn't mind letting me know. I was cat-called from the dorm room balconies and constantly asked for my number at the local internet cafes. (Yes, we didn't have internet in our dorms. We had to go to a business that had a room full of computers and pay for internet usage by the minute).

As I walked through campus from class, I would pass the dormitories, and all of them had balconies to the outside. On most days, I would receive shouts from the men. It would start off with a simple shout of *obruni*, which in twi (the tribal language spoke in Accra) meant, "white person".

They would draw it out, though, as they shouted— "Oooooohhhhh-bru-niiiiii!"—as if they were animals in the wild and calling for their mate. I'm not sure how animals react to these calls in the wild, but my reaction was to ignore them. I thought ignoring them would make them realize I wasn't interested and they would back off. It did the exact opposite.

After a few long "obruni" shouts, the men translated their shouts into English, most likely thinking I just didn't understand them. They were wrong. They would shout, "Hey, white girl!"

Again, I ignored their calls, hoping they would stop. In my head I shouted back, *I knew what you said the first time, dude. I'm ignoring you!* I'd also pick up my walking speed at this point, thinking eventually they would stop when they couldn't see me. Sometimes they would give up, but you know there are always those guys who never give up. Those guys would pursue other creative techniques in the English language and culture. They'd shout, "Hey Shakira! Shake those hips!" or "Hey, Britney Spears!" I'll admit, the creative shouts got some laughs from me, but definitely not my number.

I've never liked when guys were aggressive with me. It usually pushed me away. The shouting from the balconies definitely pushed me away. Instead, I found interest in the guys who were experiencing the same foreign-traveler experience as me. I found a guy in a group of friends I had grown close to during my first weeks there and would continue to stay close with even to this day (thank you, social media).

The group was a couple of Americans, a couple of Canadians, and the rest were Norwegian. The Norwegians all spoke perfect English and were hilarious. Most of them had traveled before, and a couple of them had lived in Lebanon for a year and spoke a little Arabic. I was very impressed and loved hanging out with them. There was only one Norwegian guy in the group. He was a little quiet, but really nice.

Mr. Norwegian and I spent a little time together. We went to a reggae dance party on the beach and toured a botanical garden, too. But everything we did was in a group. We never really spent any alone time together. He was a nice side distraction, but I wasn't really looking to date anyone during the trip. I really wanted to focus on meeting as many people as I could and learning as much about the country and about myself as I could. He was a fun dance and travel partner, but nothing really happened between us. Not even a kiss. We were fleeting crushes who just flirted with each other when we hung out in groups. It was fun. It was innocent. That's as far as it went.

We took great photos together, but we were nothing more of a couple than what you saw in those photos. (I could say the same about a lot of couple-photos I've seen on social media nowadays.) I've stayed friends with him, though. He's a great guy, and one day, he's going to make a great boyfriend or husband to someone else.

He will always be a great friend to me. I think he felt the same about me. He never pursued me and he never asked me out. We both just enjoyed each other's company, knowing that we would be going back to our separate countries—miles and miles away from each other—in just a couple months. Sometimes you have those meet-ups. Those crushes who will always just be crushes in that time, in that moment. But, hopefully, if you're lucky, they become your friends for more than just that moment. I was lucky enough and got to see Mr. Norwegian in Norway years later. There was still nothing more than just a crush between us, but we'll always be friends, and I'm very thankful for that.

Mr. Italiano

I'll admit that wanting to travel and be single in Africa wasn't the only reason I didn't want to date Mr. Norwegian. My heart was still holding on and yearning for a man back in my home country. Mr. Italiano was still very much in my mind, my heart, and all over my Facebook. No matter how far you are from someone, social media can make you think you're much closer.

Mr. Italiano would send me messages and comment on all of the photos I posted. As much as I was hoping not to forget him, he seemed to be making sure I definitely wouldn't forget him. In the beginning he gave me a lot of attention, but as the months drew on, he grew more and more distant. I learned he had a girlfriend, but it didn't bother me. I really believed I shared something special with him and I didn't mind that he was dating someone else. I didn't think it would really last.

As my time in Ghana was coming to a close, I was finding myself making plans to see Mr. Italiano when I landed in Chicago. He had tickets to a Cubs' game and he wanted to see me. I was excited to get back to

America and I was really excited to see him. He had broken up with his girlfriend, as I knew he would. We had lasted my four months away (as friends, anyway) and now we were going to be in the same city.

I landed in Chicago and my parents and college roommate, SisterWhoWantsMyMister (you'll learn later how she got this name), were both there to meet me. I saw my parents for a little bit and went to say hi to my friends before I headed back home to Ohio for the summer. Specifically, I went to see Mr. Italiano.

My heart was racing as I rode the El train to Wrigley field, where my roommate and I were going to meet him for the Cubs' game. We flirted all night, and I had a great time. He seemed just as excited to see me as I was to see him. We flirted and took cute pictures together. I felt like the time apart was good for both of us. We both had a chance to see how important each of us was to the other.

One of my favorite quotes seemed to be coming true. "People never know how special someone is until they leave, but maybe sometimes it's important to leave, so they are given that chance to see how special that someone really is…" -Ali Nitka

I went back home that summer thinking I had found a great guy, and I was going to have a great boyfriend starting off my junior year. We stayed in contact a little over the summer, and it flew by. I spent a few weeks back home working my old summer job and visiting with my family. I saw TheNextDoorNeighbor a couple of times, but nothing like the first summer I shared with him. Then I spent the rest of the summer interning and living in Washington D.C.

I didn't pursue or date any new guys I met that summer. I don't think I really let myself. I was too concerned with getting back to Chicago and seeing Mr. Italiano. There was also no one I met at the time that took my mind off Mr. Italiano. I focused more on learning about what I wanted to do with my life. I learned I didn't want to work in politics, and definitely not politics in D.C. I could at least check that off my list.

The One Who Shows You How You Should Be Treated

I was in D.C. for a summer internship with an Illinois State Representative and college courses all taught by Marquette University professors. The program was mostly attended by students from Marquette and one other girl from Loyola. We all stayed in apartment buildings close to the Hill, donated by former Marquette alumni, and were assigned an internship with a member of the House or Senate.

We learned all about how politics were handled on the hill and gave tours of the Capitol building to constituents who were in town visiting. If you've ever visited D.C. and were given a tour by a college student, you should know some of the facts told to you that day were most likely exaggerated or completely made up. As I gave tours, I would hear others giving stories I had not heard before. It at least made for an interesting time.

I grew close with all of my classmates on that trip and still talk and hangout with the fellow Loyola student who shared a bunk bed with me. We would play softball in the beautiful Virginia parks and run on The Mall. (No, not a shopping mall, the National

Mall where the Washington Monument's located.) It was a short program, but I learned a ton, from learning to sail along the Potomac River to watching a filibuster argued on the Senate floor. I also learned I never wanted to work in politics. I wasn't cut out for the low salaries and slow movement of how laws were negotiated, argued, picked apart, and usually left to die before ever coming to a vote.

Along with our classroom time and internship duties, we also took time to check out all the national monuments, museums, and farmers' markets. None of us had a lot of money since we were going to school and working unpaid internships. As I was walking along a farmers' market one day with the rest of our group, I saw a bucket full of beautiful sunflowers and instantly wanted to buy one and take it home. I talked myself out of it, though. I needed to save my money for food and useful things, not plants that I'd throw out in less than a week.

I stood there for a good amount of time trying to decide if it was worth spending the money for a little brightness in my apartment. Ultimately, I talked myself out of it and hurried to catch up with the others as we returned home for the day. Just before we were to leave, though, TheOneWhoShowsYouHowYou-ShouldBeTreated stopped us and said he'd be right back. When he returned, he was carrying one of those big yellow sunflowers and handed it to me. He knew how much I had been staring at them and wanted me to have it and make my day a little better. There was nothing more between us and we were truly just friends. He was dating another girl back home and I didn't even like him as more than a friend, but he showed me exactly the type of guy I wanted to date. Sometimes you just need to be reminded that they exist and you deserve them.

Mr. Italiano

As the summer wound down, I returned back to my parents' home in Ohio for a couple weeks before heading back to Loyola. I was thankful for all of the experiences I'd had that past year, but I was ready to get back to school and stay put for a little bit. My parents drove me to the city and this time dropped me off at an off-campus apartment that I was sharing with SisterWhoWantsMyMister and her friend, My-Replacement.

I met SisterWhoWantsMyMister freshman year. She lived in the dorm room next to mine and latched on to me pretty quickly. We hung out a lot the second semester of my freshman year and roomed together the semester before I studied in Africa. She called me her sister, but she didn't treat me like one. However, just like how love can give you rose-colored glasses in a relationship, you can also become blinded in a friendship.

I trusted her, and I didn't like to fight. She would be rude at times, but I didn't think anything of it and brushed it off because I didn't want to deal with it. Eventually, I couldn't take it anymore. This semester was the breaking point. I finally took those blurry friendship glasses off and accepted the fact that she wasn't really a good friend. It took a lot, though. It took her interfering and hurting my other friendships and my love interests.

See, the thing about love and relationships is that friends, either yours or the other person's, can often times make or break it between the two of you. Usually jealousy plays a huge part in your friends interfering with a love interest. They may want to be with your love interest or they may just be jealous that they don't get to spend as much time with you. In this case, SisterWhoWantsMyMister had both forms of jealousy. She didn't like that I wasn't spending all of my time with her and she also wanted Mr. Italiano.

I've also had the firm belief that a friendship is more important than fighting over a guy. What I failed at taking into consideration was not *all* friendships are more important than fighting over a guy. Only *good* friendships are worth it. Some friendships are worth giving up on for a quality guy you care about. This friendship was one of those worth giving up. But, just like in a relationship, you usually don't see it until it's too late.

My living situation was less than comfortable. SisterWhoWantsMyMister had found an apartment for us with MyReplacement when I was living in D.C. over the summer. SisterWhoWantsMyMister was living in a suburb of Chicago with her Aunt during the summer, so it was easy for her to drive up and find something for all of us. I was excited to be living off campus. I felt like I had a little more independence without having to show my student ID to the front desk clerkswhotooktheirjobstooseriously of a dormitory and having the ability to invite whomever I wanted over whenever I wanted.

The uncomfortable part wasn't the independence, it was the apartment layout. They had rented a two-bedroom apartment, and there were three of us living there. Since I wasn't in Chicago to find the apartment, I got the short-end of the deal. Both SisterWhoWantsMyMister and MyReplacement had their own bedrooms with a single door that closed and allowed them privacy. I lived in the dining room and used the main entryway closet as my closet. I had three doors: French see-through double-doors on one wall that entered into the living room, a single door that was the entrance to SisterWhoWantsMyMister's room, and a third entryway entrance with no door at all, just a curtain on a cheap curtain rod. I had zero privacy, and as I'd learn, SisterWhoWantsMyMister wanted it that way.

When I was gone, I had requested that Mr. Italiano look out for SisterWhoWantsMyMister and make sure he did things with her so she wouldn't get lonely. He obliged as a courtesy for me, and she took advantage of the situation. When I returned, he and his friends were now texting her. So were many of my other guy friends. It was a hard pill to swallow, but I had been gone for a semester and a summer. It made sense that my friends and Mr. Italiano had become closer with her. It wouldn't have been a big deal, but SisterWhoWantsMyMister made it a big deal.

She would continue to brag to me how Mr. Italiano was texting her. How Mr. Italiano wanted us to meet him. At first I brushed it off, blaming my own jealousy for my frustrations with hearing that he was texting her a lot. He had invited us both to a back-to-school house party at his new apartment in Wrigleyville. He called it the "penthouse," and he lived with his friends from high school who went to a neighboring college. This "penthouse" was more like a frat house located on the bottom floor of a two-floor apartment house with neon beer themed lights hanging on the walls.

I was really excited to see Mr. Italiano that night and dressed to impress him. I had on tight jeans that left nothing to the imagination, high heels, and a tight strapless top. I wanted him to notice me. I wanted him to want me. Unfortunately, I wouldn't be the only girl at the party to want him to want them. Another girl was going to be even more of a distraction and interference between me and Mr. Italiano than SisterWhoWantsMyMister.

That night, one of Mr. Italiano's friends picked SisterWhoWantsMyMister and me up from our apartment and drove us to the party. (It's much easier to see your crush when you have an entourage.) We quickly parked and headed up to the apartment building. My heart felt like it was beating outside my chest. It was a mixture of excitement and nervousness. I hadn't seen him since I got back from Ghana. I didn't know what was going to happen, but I felt like that night was going to finally provide me answers to all my questions.

I had already taken a shot of liquid courage to help my confidence. I strutted into the house with what I thought was a sexy, confident walk. You know, picturing in your head those models walking down the runway, hoping your body is replicating the image. I wanted him to notice me as soon as I walked in. I wanted his friends to notice me, too. The party was in full swing when we walked in and most of the people were pretty drunk. So, my walk did little to draw anyone's attention, including Mr. Italiano's.

There were quite a lot of people and quite a lot of small rooms. We had to maneuver our way through the drunken party maze to find him.

Once we found him, I could tell he'd had a lot to drink. He smiled at me and gave me a hug, but he seemed really nervous, which made me feel a little bit better about my own anxiety of seeing him. I thought for sure it was a good sign that he was nervous. I thought it meant he was interested in me.

He made his round of hugs in the group and then excitedly showed us his new home for the year and introduced us to his roommates. He showed us where we could grab drinks in the kitchen and ran off to talk to some other friends.

As we were in the kitchen, I noticed a girl, Ms. Desperate, staring at Mr. Italiano, who was just outside the kitchen. Ms. Desperate was laughing and talking loudly to get his attention. She wouldn't leave his side the entire night. It was really annoying me. I'm sure she annoyed him, too.

I back down in these situations. I don't like to be the annoying girl, begging for the attention from a guy. I believe that if a guy wants to be with me, he'll make the effort to give me attention without me having to jump up and down. I wasn't desperate like this girl, and I certainly wasn't about to start acting like it. I also figured if he liked a girl like that, he should date her and not me because I was never going to be that way.

We didn't stay too long at the party, and soon we were saying our goodbyes to Mr. Italiano. I was okay to leave because I was tired of watching Ms. Desperate beg for his attention. The night did not go how I had hoped it would go. It did give me clarity, though. Mr. Italiano didn't seem to want to settle down and date me. I was starting to tell myself this as I exited the party. I had to accept that it wasn't going to work out.

But then, I went to hug him goodnight.

He usually gives me a kiss on either side of the check, the "Italian way" he would say. That night, we kissed on the lips. It seemed to last forever, but I know in reality it was just a quick one. I think he and I were both surprised by what had happened. It didn't seem to be an intentional kiss by either of us. I certainly wasn't looking for a kiss that night. I'd been hoping for one, but I had given up hope by that point.

We both smiled at each other and laughed a little at the incident. Our friends were yelling at me to hurry up so they could leave, so I quickly waived goodbye and ran down the front steps and jumped in the car. As we pulled away from the party, my friends all got quiet and looked at me with goofy smiles on their faces.

"What?" I said with a huge smile on my face.

One of my friends laughed. "We saw that kiss, Ashley…."

I just smiled and said, "It was an accident, he didn't mean to do it."

"Uh huh…" he said.

I spent the rest of the night wondering if my friend had a point. Did Mr. Italiano actually mean to kiss me? Was this his way to get my attention and let me know he wanted to date me? The party did not give me any answers. Instead, it gave me more questions. It's how most of my dating life has gone and will go. So many questions. Especially one:

Why does it have to be so difficult?

My brother always says to me, "Ashley, it should just be easy."

And I completely agree. It *should* be easy. You should be able to hang out with a guy. Tell each other you like each other. Then date. Boom. Unfortunately, it's just not that easy for a lot of people. Including myself.

Instead, you hang out a lot with another person. Neither of you say anything to each other until months later. Then, once you say something, your relationship with the other person all of a sudden blows up in your face. You were wrong about everything. You were wrong about all the flirting, touching, looks, comments, and hints.

Now you're really confused about dating. You question if you will ever really know when a person likes you and wants to date you. This happens over and over. Then you start building up a wall as you get older, and now everyone has to work on breaking down everyone's walls.

Blah. But I digress.

Just remember, the process above happens every single time these situations occur. You have to wipe that slate clean. Try not to bring the past with you, and try to remain open to new, hopefully easier, relationships.

After the party, things started to get much more murky. I was hanging out with Mr. Italiano and his friends at his apartment one night. He proceeded to tell us more details of the party after we had left.

He told us that Ms. Desperate had taken Mr. Italiano by the hand and pulled him into his bedroom. She then closed the door and proceeded to unbutton her pants and pull them down. (I can't make this stuff up.) He didn't help her at all. He just stood there and stared at her in disbelief.

Ladies, you should know if you're doing this with a guy, you're telling him you just want to hook up with him. You're not telling him that you want a relationship with him.

As I heard this part of the story, my heart sunk to my stomach. A lot of the men I had met at that time in my life would hookup with the girl. I didn't think Mr. Italiano was that type of guy, but I had been proven wrong before. I continued to listen to the rest of the story, hoping for the best but assuming the worst—that my chances with Mr. Italiano were over.

Mr. Italiano then proceeded to tell us that he freaked out and ran over to her and started to try and pull her pants back up. She continued to pull her pants down as he was trying to pull them up. He said his friends then threw his door open and started encouraging him to hook up with her while he was trying to tell them he was just trying to get her out of his room. He was laughing at this point at the ridiculousness of the situation. He looked my way and smiled even bigger.

I laughed even harder when he looked at me. I felt like he was looking for my reaction from the story. As if he wanted to see if I would get jealous of the other girl. That part was annoying—the game-playing. But I did feel a lot better knowing Ms. Desperate didn't win out in the end. I felt reassured that he was the good guy I thought he was and he hadn't fallen for Ms. Desperate's tactics. Maybe, just maybe, it would work out with him in the end.

If it wasn't for SisterWhoWantsMyMister, I might have actually dated Mr. Italiano. I was finally excited about Mr. Italiano and I would of course talk to my best friend, SisterWhoWantsMyMister, about him. However, as the weeks continued for the school year, she became more and more manipulative and mean. I slowly told her less and less.

I was asked to join my school's mock trial team and I started working a part time job in Evanston, a suburb of Chicago just a short train ride north of campus. I spent a lot of time at my job, in class, or at practice for mock trial. I spent less time with SisterWhoWantsMyMister, and she did not like it. Soon, I found her continuously asking me who was texting or calling my phone. She wanted to know all about my schedule and who I was hanging out with or talking to on the phone.

My bedroom had almost no privacy from her, and I certainly didn't want her to always know what else was going on in my life. Everyone needs a little privacy here and there. Soon, she would start telling me that Mr. Italiano was texting her. She would even tell me he had texted her and ask me if he had done the same to me. He hadn't.

She pushed it even more. She would tell me I should text him something like, *Hey, what are you up to today?* I thought it was harmless, so I texted him. Then she would keep asking me if he texted me back. He never did. Then she would ask if I wanted to stop by his house and bring him snacks while he was studying. I of course responded, "Um no, why would I go to his house if he won't even respond to my text?" I told her she was more than welcome to go without me. She declined.

I didn't understand what was going on with her, but I knew it wasn't in my best interest. By November, I would found out. It was all sparked by a Facebook comment. Imagine if social media never existed. I may have never discovered everything. Social media can be terrible on one hand, with people lying about themselves behind the screen of a computer, but also helpful on the other hand, helping you find out people's secrets.

I was in class downtown and came out to several missed calls from my sister (my real biological sister who doesn't want my mister). She left me a voicemail and sounded really upset and stressed out. She didn't go into details about what happened. She just asked me to call her back.

"What's going on?" I asked my sister, really concerned.

"Do you know a Mr. Italiano? What is his problem?"

My mouth dropped open. My mind was filled with a thousand thoughts—*What did he do? Why was he bothering my sister? Screw him! Don't mess with my family!* I asked her what happened. She explained that she had posted on her Facebook wall about the name she'd chosen for my nephew who had yet to be born. He was also her first child. Mr. Italiano felt the need to comment on that post about the name. He said something about how the name was dumb and asked why anyone would name their kid by that name.

I was pissed. Super pissed. It's one thing to mess with me, but messing with my sister was not okay. Especially about the name *she* chose for her first child. That's just wrong.

I apologized to her and told her I would take care of it. I hung up the phone with her and immediately called Mr. Italiano. In this moment, I didn't care about having a relationship with him anymore. I didn't care if I hurt his feelings or if he never wanted to date me after we talked. All I cared about was fixing the situation and making my sister feel better.

He didn't pick up his phone. I think he knew. I left him a voicemail. "What the hell is your problem? Why would you post on my sister's Facebook about my nephew's name? Why would you do that? It's one thing to pick on me or tease me. It's another thing to make fun of a name my sister chose for her first-born. I don't know what your problem is, but you need to remove that comment immediately and apologize to my sister." I hung up.

I called my sister back and let her know that I told him to take the post down and to apologize to her. I apologized for him, too. I felt extremely bad. I could only imagine the amount of time she took to figure out what name she wanted to give my nephew. The books she read, the websites she perused. The late-night conversations she had with her husband, going back and forth on what name she should choose. How she finally decided on the name. How she was excited to share it with her family and friends and celebrate it. How when she finally did share it, Mr. Italiano (a man she'd never met) felt the need to criticize her for it.

Mr. Italiano eventually contacted me back. He half-apologized for his comment. He did remove it. He didn't accept full blame, though. He told me how it wasn't a big deal and he didn't know it was my sister since she had her married name on Facebook. Blah, blah, blah. Even if it wasn't my sister, what he did was messed up. You don't criticize a first-time mom on the name she chooses for her child. Especially as a comment on *her* social media page.

The ridiculous thing about it was that the name wasn't even weird. It was normal. In fact, it was one of the most popular baby names in the past ten years. I don't think it ever had to do with his name. I do think Mr. Italiano knew she was my sister. I think he wanted to get my attention. Well, he did. But he got the wrong type of my attention. I was mad at him. He was going to have to really work hard to change my opinion of him.

But, like I said, this was just the catalyst to an explosion of events. Next up, Mr. Italiano was going to tell me all the things he'd been holding back for the past couple of months. All the things that were sparked and encouraged by SisterWhoWantsMyMister's conversations with him. Conversations I was unaware of.

My class was at the downtown Loyola campus, and I lived about a forty-five-minute bus ride north of it. I jumped on the downtown Chicago city bus to ride it back up north to my apartment. I had an old-school phone back then and didn't have data to surf the internet, so I wasn't able to check my Facebook during the trip. I listened to some music on my iPod and tried to distract myself from everything that just happened. How quickly a night can turn from any other night to a night of drama.

I got off the bus at the Rogers Park bus stop closest to my apartment and casually walked home. I went directly to my room and opened up my computer to check on the status of the Facebook fiasco. I wanted to make sure Mr. Italiano removed his comment and apologized to my sister.

I checked the post, and he had removed his comment. I was happy he no longer had the comment on my sister's post. Then I got an email. It was from Mr. Italiano. I saved it. I printed it out and saved it. I still have it to this day. To remind me of that night. To remind me about what type of person he was. I wish I could say that it was a reminder I took seriously every day after receiving it. Unfortunately, I didn't.

The letter told me how he had removed me from Facebook as a friend and how he was repulsed by me and my pursuit of him. That's right, he actually used the word "repulsed." How I'd told his friends and SisterWhoWantsMyMister I was enamored with his family. How I constantly talked to all of his friends and SisterWhoWantsMyMister about my relationship issues with him. How I was completely different from what he wanted in a girlfriend or future wife. How we had different ideals of religion and family. He told me he had tried to warn me and push me away, but I had left him with no other choice but to write me that letter and remove me from his friend group.

The letter was a whole page. A whole page telling me how terrible of a person I was and how terrible of a friend I was. I became more and more angry as I read each sentence. I also became more and more confused. I didn't know what he was talking about. I had discussed my interest in him with SisterWhoWantsMyMister a couple times, but not too much. Especially since he seemed to distance himself from me.

I remembered telling SisterWhoWantsMyMister at some point in the first month back to school that I was upset several of my guy friends were contacting her about parties and not me. It was hard for me to realize that my friends had grown closer with her when I was studying abroad. I apologized to SisterWhoWantsMyMister about it, though. I realized it wasn't her fault and I would have to work on building those relationships back up on my own.

I also didn't understand why he thought I was pursuing him so hardcore. I barely texted him and I hadn't asked to hang out with him for weeks. I had actually started to develop feelings for a couple of other guys and I had started hanging out with them more since I didn't think Mr. Italiano was interested in dating me.

I told him all of this. I wrote him an entire-page letter in response. I explained how confused I was by everything he was saying. How I had every right to be upset with him about what he said to my sister. How I didn't appreciate the way he handled the situation. How I needed some time to cool down.

It took him a couple days, but he started to realize that maybe he was misled by things people were saying to him. Mainly things coming from SisterWhoWantsMyMister. He requested my friendship on Facebook again. I ignored it. I wasn't ready to be friends with him again. I didn't want to be friends with someone who would say those things to me, or even believe those things about me. Which pissed him off, again. He certainly had that Italian-anger thing down.

Eventually I did add him back on Facebook. I kept my guard up, though. I didn't trust anyone in his friendship group anymore, and I definitely didn't trust SisterWhoWantsMyMister. I threw myself into extracurricular activities, my studies, and my job. I tried to fill my time with distractions so I didn't even have a second to think about what was going on with Mr. Italiano, Mr. Italiano's friends, or SisterWhoWantsMyMister. I needed some space. I needed some time to think about whether or not I even wanted to be friends with Mr. Italiano, let alone pursue a relationship with him.

Mr. FakeFacebookRelationship

During this time, I had another male distraction—
Mr. FakeFacebookRelationship. After my Facebook
relationship-status fiasco with Mr.
TooMuchTooSoon, I decided I didn't want to leave
my Facebook status on single. I didn't really want the
Facebook world to know my true relationship status.
At the time, I was required to set some sort of status. I
had three choices: "Single," "In a Relationship
with…," or "In a Complicated Relationship with…."
I wanted choice number three. My love life was
complicated. Yes, I was single. But it was more
complicated than "single."

I selected "In a Complicated Relationship with…"
and asked my friend Mr. FakeFacebookRelationship
to join me in this I. He joyfully agreed. I now had a
Facebook relationship I was satisfied with; if someone
really wanted to date me, they would have to get to
know me in person instead of stalking my Facebook
profile page.

The thing was, I started to develop feelings for Mr.
FakeFacebookRelationship. He was a great guy and
one of my best friends at Loyola. That's the type of

relationship I wanted. I wanted to date my best friend, my partner in crime. He was a separate love interest from Mr. Italiano. He seemed like he would treat me better than Mr. Italiano. But I wasn't sure Mr. FakeFacebookRelationship felt the same way about me.

I told Mr. Italiano about my interest in Mr. FakeFacebookRelationship in the letter. I explained how I had interest in dating a few guys in addition to Mr. Italiano. That the reason I didn't confront Mr. Italiano about my feelings for him was because I wasn't sure which relationship I wanted to pursue. This was also a reason Mr. Italiano started to take a few steps back from his initial aggressive attack on me and his assumptions that I was a crazy, obsessed girl who only wanted to date him. (Some people can be so self-absorbed.) It also makes me wonder about all those times guys have told me their exes are crazy. Were they really crazy? Or was that all in the guys' heads?

Mr. Italiano

I slowly let Mr. Italiano back into my life, more so because I liked his friends than because I wanted him back in my life. It took time. I really kept my distance from him. I pursued Mr. FakeFacebookRelationship, but neither of us really made a move to let the other know about our feelings. We flirted. We hung out. But we never got past that "friend" title. Maybe it had something to do with our fake Facebook relationship. Maybe we could never let our guards down and get past the relationship joke to have a real one. Maybe we just weren't meant to be together.

As much as I tried to stay away from Mr. Italiano, fate had other ideas for us. I specifically moved to Chicago for many reasons. One of those reasons? So I could live in a city big enough to never run into people when I didn't want to see them. Chicago is the third largest city in the country, and I still managed to run into people I didn't want to see. One of those times was right before Thanksgiving break.

Mr. Italiano and his friends (including SisterWhoWantsMyMister) were all meeting up to celebrate one of his friend's birthdays. They were doing a whole evening where they were going to surprise him and take him out. I couldn't go. I was going home not only for Thanksgiving, but also for my cousin's wedding. She had asked me to read at her wedding. I apologized for not being able to attend my friends' gathering, but relieved I had a legitimate excuse to not have to see Mr. Italiano.

I was riding the train back from one of my last classes to head back to my apartment, pack up, and head on up to my other cousin's house so we could drive back to Ohio together. I was relaxed and happy to see family after all the drama. I wanted to forget about it all and be surrounded by my loving family. Sometimes that's all you need to feel better: some family time.

I had picked up a *Red Eye* newspaper and was reading one of the editorials when I felt the pressure of someone leaning into my personal space. Whoever it was pushed into my outstretched paper. I figured they just lost their balance. It was easy to do on the train. The conductors sped through each line and braked hard at each stop. Plus there were a lot of turns and the trains were pretty old. Then it happened again. This time the train wasn't jostling at all. Rude.

The third time it happened, I got pissed. *Okay, now the person is doing it on purpose*. Based on the usual clientele on the train, I was ready for an inappropriate male to be on the other side as I lowered my paper. Some guy that would give me some inappropriate comment. To my surprise, it was Mr. Italiano. Woah. I was completely caught off guard. I hadn't actually seen him face-to-face since the whole fiasco. We had chatted a little here and there online, but not face-to-face.

"Oh, hey," I said, too surprised to express my retained anger for him. I laughed and told him I thought he was some creeper trying to hit on me. The irony wasn't seeing him on the train. Those things tend to happen every once in a while, especially when we all go to the same school and usually traverse the same public transportation lines. No, the strange thing about it all was how he ended up on that train.

He told me he was on his way to meet the birthday friend and accidentally took the wrong train. He got on the south train but needed the north train. If you don't pay attention, this can easily happen. So he had just happened to get off at that stop to get back on the train and head back north. He just happened to get on the car I was sitting in. Just plain weird. I thought about this as we said our goodbyes and he left the train.

I'm a believer in serendipity. I believe things happen for a reason, and if you're meant to be with someone, it will happen. Maybe if I didn't believe in those things my life would've taken a different path, or maybe I wouldn't have spent so much time thinking the universe had plans for me to be with Mr. Italiano. Who knows? But in that moment, I questioned whether I was supposed to forgive him and this was just a test or if I was truly supposed to walk away from any type of friendship with him. Was the universe telling me there was something more?

As I said before, men always come back. Whether it's serendipity or they realize they messed up, I'll never know. But they come back. It's up to you to decide whether you want to take them back.

This was our first big fight. It wouldn't be our last fight. Nope. We had a lot of fights. A lot. Most of them were about him being mad at me for things he had heard instead of just talking to me. He would blow up and take it out on me. Looking back, I have no idea why I decided to waste so much time thinking about him, why I ever had feelings for him, or why I continued to have feelings for him. I never told him about my feelings when I actually had them, either. I just kept going with the flow.

I got to my cousin's house, excited to leave Chicago for a little bit and rejuvenate with my family. I have a pretty big family on both sides. My mom is one of six kids and my dad one of seven. I'm an extrovert and gain so much energy from groups, especially groups of people I care about and love. Whenever something is going wrong in my love life, a trip to visit family always makes me feel better. I'm so grateful for that in my life. I've also developed some close friendships that can do the same. Don't underestimate the love of your family and friends. It can do wonders for your soul.

When I returned to school after Thanksgiving break, there were only a couple weeks left before winter break. Those weeks were full of studying and exams. It was also just a short time before I headed off to the United Kingdom with my family for Christmas and New Year's. My brother had spent the semester living in Scotland, and my parents, grandparents, and uncle were all flying out to meet him, to celebrate the holidays.

It was such a short amount of time crammed with so many things that needed done. There didn't even seem to be much time for more boy drama. But if there is a will, there is a way. So sure enough, there was one more incident before I left the country for the holidays.

SisterWhoWantsMyMister was no longer okay with me spending all my time outside of the apartment. At this point, I woke up at 7:00 a.m., took the train to my job, went to class, then to the library, and studied until 2:00 a.m. I spent as little time in my apartment as possible. What really set her off was when I asked to move my room to a small front room without a door. I wanted to move there because it only had one entrance compared to the three in the dining room. Plus, that one entrance wasn't the bedroom door of SisterWhoWantsMyMister.

I wanted my privacy. SisterWhoWantsMyMister didn't want me to have any privacy, nor did she want me to get something I wanted. She pushed back, stating it was where they kept plants and relaxed. I was done being polite. *Who the hell cares about plants when I feel super uncomfortable and have no privacy? I think I have more rights to the room than some dumb plant.*

I tried to handle things the right way. You know, ask for permission first since it's a shared apartment. I thought I was reasonable with my request and I was just trying to be polite. The reasons for why they thought I shouldn't move rooms were ridiculous. At this point, I was so stressed out without privacy that I was concerned for my grades. I didn't care what my roommates wanted anymore. I requested the help of a friend and moved all my stuff one night when I knew they'd be gone. Sometimes it's true what they say, it's better to ask for forgiveness than permission. (Especially, when you've already tried to get permission!)

This move started a *huge* fight with SisterWhoWants-MyMister, and MyReplacement now had reason to join in on the hate train. I left the apartment to study more in the library and avoid seeing my roommates come home to the change. I knew they wouldn't move it back, but I did not expect what happened next. I came home to find all the living-room furniture shoved into the small dining room where I used to sleep. It was intentionally placed as a way of restricting my use of the TV and couches. I didn't care, though. I was rarely in our apartment and didn't even watch the TV.

I couldn't wait for winter break at this point. I felt really uncomfortable in my own home and I could barely sleep. I had a flimsy wooden wall divider protecting me from them at night. I didn't trust them at all anymore, and I didn't know what they would do when I was asleep.

On top of my terrible living conditions, I'd received a call from Mr. Italiano. He told me he'd heard I wasn't treating SisterWhoWantsMyMister very well and I needed to be kinder to her because her parents had just gone through a divorce the year before. I responded to him with an, "Are you kidding me!?" I told him how I hadn't done anything but move my stuff because I didn't feel comfortable anymore and how she was the one causing all of the problems. How I didn't want to even live in my apartment anymore. He laughed. He didn't believe a word I said.

I broke down. I cried. I felt completely defeated. She had won. She had won him over and I assumed she probably won his friends over with him. I gave up right then. I stopped trying to talk to SisterWho-WantsMyMister, My Replacement, Mr. Italiano, or any of his friends. I dove into my studies and prepared for a trip overseas. I didn't care any more. I told myself (and yelled it through our front apartment door one day at SisterWhoWantsMyMister) that "if they're my true friends then they'll see me for who I am and not believe all the things you're saying."

I was right, too. It didn't happen right away, but SisterWhoWantsMyMister showed her true colors to Mr. Italiano and his friends. I stepped away and let them see it for themselves. Remember to do that in situations. Sometimes it's important to step away from a group and let them see for themselves someone's true colors. Actions speak much louder than your words in these situations. If they still don't believe you and listen to your friend and don't see you for who you truly are, they're not good friends and you should move on.

Mr. Italiano and his friends saw SisterWhoWants-MyMister's true colors on New Year's Eve that year. She had invited them all down to our apartment to bring in the New Year. Only she actually just wanted Mr. Italiano, and Mr. Italiano bailed for a family thing. She ended up leaving them outside in the cold and ignored their phone calls. She later made up some story about passing out and not hearing their calls. They didn't believe her.

Slowly, one by one, they came back to be my friends. Mr. Italiano was last, but he did return. In the meantime, I focused on competing for Loyola in mock trial competitions. (I know, I'm a huge dork.) I also started to see one of my fellow teammates as more than just a friend. I'm going to call him Mr. SmoothTalker. He just had a way of making you like him just by his speeches. His words rolled of his tongue like molasses and he left you wanting to hear more. At least, that's what his words did to me.

Mr. SmoothTalker

You know those types of people in the world—the type who can hold the attention of any large group by their tone, their voice, and their words. Mr. SmoothTalker was one of those people. He was pretty awkward outside those speeches, though. He dressed in either a professional suit or a relaxed look in jeans and a t-shirt. There was no in between. He was Italian-American. Those Italians, no matter what percentage… they just always seem to pull me in for some reason.

I think Mr. Italiano was a little jealous of Mr. SmoothTalker. See, Mr. Italiano is only a small percentage Italian. This wasn't so for Mr. SmoothTalker. He was full-on Italian and cooked like it, too. He would make his own homemade spaghetti sauce and very much looked the part, with dark hair and features.

Mr. SmoothTalker didn't play games. He liked me, and I liked him. We did our best to hide our relationship from the rest of our mock trial team, but we're pretty bad at hiding those things. Plus, my team was good at investigating. It wasn't hard for them to spot hints and evidence to discover our hidden affair. He wouldn't be the only relationship I tried to hide from the public. I've come to learn over the years it's not always worth it. Privacy is one thing, but hiding your feelings for someone from the public could also be hiding issues you're not willing to confront within your relationship. Hiding issues wasn't a thing with Mr. SmoothTalker, but it would end up being a coverup excuse for a different guy I dated in grad school.

I told Mr. Italiano and his friends about Mr. SmoothTalker. They told me I could do better. (This would be a common theme in my life: my friends telling me I could do better than a guy I was interested in, but never really giving me an example of a guy I should be dating). I didn't care what they thought, though. (Per usual.) Mr. SmoothTalker was a gentleman. More than that, he liked me and he actually did something about it by dating me. Unlike Mr. Italiano, who was all talk and no show. I also think my new relationship made Mr. Italiano realize I wasn't as obsessed with him as SisterWhoWantsMyMister made it out to seem.

I spent the rest of my junior year of college hanging out with my mock trial team and Mr. SmoothTalker. I spent less time with Mr. Italiano and his friends. I still didn't fully trust them all. I did my best to avoid SisterWhoWantsMyMister and turned to other friends who didn't try to destroy my relationships or friendships.

I enjoyed late night movies and pizza time with Mr. SmoothTalker. Soon, the school year was ending and summer was just around the corner. Mr. SmoothTalker was graduating that year. His family lived nearby, and I didn't really think about what would happen to us after graduation. I was just living in the moment with him and enjoying the time we had together.

I planned for him to come into the city and go out with me and some of my friends at the end of the school year. I had moved out of the apartment I had shared with SisterWhoWantsMyMister and MyReplacement. I found a subletter and moved into one of my friend's apartments while she was gone for the summer. I was so excited to get out of the toxic apartment environment and enjoy a lively summer in Chicago. I had found a job in the suburbs, and a lot of my close friends were staying in the city, too.

Chicago comes alive in the summer. There are only a few months of beautiful sunshine and warm weather, and Chicagoans try to take advantage of every minute of it. I was waiting in this new apartment for Mr.

SmoothTalker to let me know he was back in the city so I could meet him outside the apartment building and let him inside.

I didn't hear from him and started to wonder what happened. I texted him. No answer. I called him. Still no answer. I sent a few more texts. Nothing. I decided to head out. I figured he might be busy doing something and would get back to me. He didn't. He didn't text me back for an entire week. Nothing.

When he finally contacted, me he explained what had happened. He was making an important life decision and he didn't want me to influence it. He wanted to decide for himself. I told him I understood, but that all he had to do was say exactly that. He just had to tell me he was trying to make an important life decision and wanted space to decide it on his own. That he didn't want me to know all the details, but he wanted time to think. I would have happily let him have the time. I would've understood.

As soon as I told him that, it's like he had an epiphany. "Oh! Yeah, I guess I could've just said that to you." I was beyond annoyed and hurt. I thought it was really rude for him to not show up and ignore me for a week. It would be a different situation if he had been injured and in the hospital, unable to communicate. But he could communicate, he just chose not to.

Here's some advice: want a good relationship with someone? Communication is key, people. You're going to have go through difficult things in life and have difficult conversations. If you keep everything bottled up inside, someone is going to get hurt. Either you or your partner. Also, if you do want space and time to think about things, that's completely fine, but let your partner know—we're not mind-readers!

So some of you may be thinking I wrote Mr. SmoothTalker off and told him to hit the road, perhaps judging me a little and thinking I should give people a second chance and that everyone makes mistakes. Listen, I agree with you. Also, I didn't end it with him. I *did* give him a second chance. I agree with you, everyone does make mistakes and it's good to talk it out and work through it instead of just giving up. So, no, that's not why I'm single (that I'm too picky, and the minute something goes wrong, I run).

I told Mr. SmoothTalker I would like him to communicate better with me the next time he needed space. He agreed to work on it, and was happy we could continue our relationship together. The decision he was making was whether or not to attend grad school or take a year off and work on a political campaign. Either decision put him somewhat close to me. One was located in Chicago and the other was located in the suburbs. I didn't really think either would put a strain on our relationship, and honestly wouldn't have encouraged him to do anything but follow his heart. His decision, however, did happen to end our relationship. Looking back now, though, I'm pretty sure either one would've caused our demise.

If you've never worked on a political campaign, you should know it takes up a lot of time. Not only for the candidate, but for all the individuals working to get votes for the candidate. You're calling people, knocking on doors, writing speeches, and supporting the candidate any way you can. As the campaign ramped up, I would call Mr. SmoothTalker to catch up with him and keep our relationship going.

He usually answered my calls, but the conversations were mainly about what he was doing on the campaign and didn't last very long. I started to notice something, too. I was the only one making the calls in our relationship. I felt like I was the only one doing the work to keep us together. I decided to test it out. What would happen if I no longer made an effort to call or text him? I'm sure you guessed it. He never reached out. Nothing. Not even a text. Until…November.

What's November? It's election month. I had a feeling that's when he would finally try to reconnect with me. I had given up calling him in July. I didn't want to continue a one-sided relationship. I didn't want to be the only one making an effort for us to stay together.

It was around November first or second. His job had pretty much finished up. The campaigning was coming to an end as voters went to their respective precincts to submit their votes. It was then I received a text message while over at a friend's apartment for a party. He texted to apologize and ask for us to get back together. He missed me and wanted to try and make things work.

Here's the thing, though: He loved politics. He eventually wanted to become a politician one day. I had already lived that life growing up in my small town of Ohio. I walked the parades, knocked on doors, and participated in commercials to help my dad win local positions. It was interesting and fun, but not something I wanted to do with my life.

I knew if I continued my relationship with him and we ended up together, my life would consist of campaign dinners, parades, and public criticism. At the time, and honestly still at this moment, I didn't want the life of a politician's wife. I give those women and men a lot of credit. They put as much work into a candidate's campaign as the candidate does him or herself.

I politely declined his offer. I also didn't appreciate it coming to me via text. Come on, men! Even a phone call would've been more personal and meaningful. But times have changed; a lot of my future relationship conversations would be done via text. It's easier, faster, and less emotional. It's a cop-out, if you ask me.

It took him four months to reach out to me. I figured if he could go four months without contacting me, he would do it again. He would just get busy with something else in his life and I would once again fall to the wayside. I didn't want to be in a one-sided relationship with someone; I wanted to be with someone who would actually make me a priority in his life. I sent a *no thank you* text response and closed that relationship in my mind.

It wasn't hard to move on from him. I had already grieved the loss months prior when he stopped contacting me. I had already said my goodbyes and I wasn't looking to re-open those wounds. It was on to the next guy and back to celebrating my final year of undergrad.

TheOneYourFamilyWantsYouToMarry

I had finished my lease with SisterWhoWants-MyMister and MyReplacement. I was finally free from them and their drama. A friend from mock trial welcomed me into her dorm room to finish out my final year in college. (My parents made me move back to campus after the terrible year off campus. I mean, I get where they're coming from, and I ended up having a great senior year!) We shared a large studio room on the first floor of a dorm building just a block from the red line train stop.

I spent the year finishing up my studies and working hard to graduate with honors, spending a lot of my time working two jobs and enjoying the ability to drink legally in the city. There wasn't anyone special in my life anymore and the previous men had all graduated and moved out of the neighborhood. No way of running into them on campus. I lived it up.

As I finished up the year, I focused more on what I was doing after school than who I should date. After taking a study course and a couple LSAT exams, I scored pretty averagely. But taking time off between school and graduate school seemed like a bad decision for me. I didn't think I'd go back to school if I had the opportunity to take a break. In retrospect, I think a break would have been very beneficial for me.

I was also debating between going to law school or pursuing a career in physical therapy or something else. After realizing the health route would require me to take a lot more science classes, and I was already behind on the application process, I decided to continue on my path to law school. I applied to several schools and was admitted to three. Two of them were in Ohio and one was in Chicago. I would spend a lot of my time that year deciding which one would be the best to attend. In the meantime, I was excited to have options and continued to relax a little more knowing I had a path to take next year.

I spent my winter break rekindling my relationship with TheNextDoorNeighbor. He was attending one of the law schools where I had been admitted. It was a fun winter friendship and nothing more. He also let me know a little bit more about law school and what it was like as a student. There was also a different relationship that was sparked by my hometown return for the holidays. His name is TheOneYourFamilyWants-YouToMarry.

He was the all-American guy, loved by pretty much anyone who met him. He was outgoing, caring, wicked smart, and cute. My family had been friends with his family since well before I was born. My uncles had attended school with his dad, and we had a long history between our two families. He was four years older than me, though. So nothing really happened between us growing up. There was too much time between us and we never really attended the same school at the same time (or at least not the same area of the school).

Our interactions growing up before college were mainly at dance competitions and recitals. His younger sister was also a student at a nearby dance school. I transferred to the dance school when I was in eighth grade. Still, he was the older brother who teased me, nothing more. Until now. I had matured, and so had he. We texted a little, and he asked me to hang out at his house and come out with him and his family for a holiday dinner. I quickly accepted.

I spent an hour curling my hair and making myself up, thinking this could be the start of a very exciting relationship. He was in his final year of dental school and I was in my final year of college. Who knew what the following year would hold for us? It didn't matter at that moment; it was new and fun.

Both of our parents approved of this potentially blossoming relationship. They had all been friends for years and saw this as a great opportunity to continue and potentially strengthen familial connections through marriage. I excitedly went out to dinner with them all and laughed most of the night. They're a warm and friendly family that makes you feel right at home.

Usually if a relationship with someone is just a fling or not meant to be, then this is where the story would end. A dinner on winter break. A fun night out, both of us caught up in the moment. That night wasn't the end of our story, though. It's never that clear. There's always something that brings the guy back into my life. It's as if they think I might be "the one," and they don't want to give up or let me go. This pattern has caused me a lot of heartache.

I wish I could tell you there are signs to look out for when you're dating these types of people. But I truly believe there's no way to know for sure. You have to put your guard down and give it your all in order to really know if you're not meant to be together. Now, some men do show you their real intentions and feelings early; others take time. TheOneYourFamily-WantsYouToMarry was one who took time.

He drove me home that night and we shared an innocent kiss on the cheeks (not even on the lips!) in my driveway. I left his car that night smiling and happy. I knew we weren't done. We had made mention of spending more time with each other before we returned to our respective schools. I also began to question whether my parents knew better than I did, and maybe he was the one guy I was supposed to marry.

My parents were still up when I arrived. They wanted to know how the date went. They seemed just as excited as me. I'm not very good at hiding my emotions, so they could easily see how great of a time I'd had at dinner. I also didn't hide from them how much fun I'd had. I told them it was a great night but I was tired, and went to bed.

As I grew older, I learned to keep a lot of details from a good date to myself. I just didn't want to jinx it. All my past relationships had ended because I excitedly talked about them with others. I thought maybe if I kept the details to myself it would work out. I also didn't want to get my parents' hopes up if it wasn't going to work out. It just made it that much harder for me to get over a relationship.

They would want to know what happened and why a relationship didn't continue. The thing was, so did I. I wanted to know why it all quickly ended. I didn't have an answer for myself, nor did I have one for them. It was the usual, "I just don't like you anymore," or, "We didn't have chemistry." There's not usually one thing or explanation. It just didn't work out.

Before I left for school, we reunited one last time for New Year's Eve. I went over to his family's house to watch the ball drop. It was a fun night full of laughter again. I felt like I fit in so easily with the family, not just with him. It was exactly what I wanted. I wanted the guy I would end up marrying to not only be a part of my family, but for me to be a part of his.

It was one of those nights where you look around and think, "I could really be a part of this family." It was easy, as my brother always told me relationships should be. I could be myself with them. (Another thing to look for when trying to find someone to date.) It all seemed to be falling into place. We exchanged another kiss on the cheek that night, bringing in the new year. We were both still nervous and shy about what was happening. Maybe a new love was beginning along with the new year? Who knew?

As I left his house that night, promises were exchanged to reconnect once we were both back in our separate cities completing the school year. Only time would tell whether either of us would make good on those words. I traveled back to Chicago to finish out my final semester of college. It was time to live it up. My grades were almost final and I was ready to enjoy my last few months in the city.

At this point in my life, I was more concerned with enjoying life and celebrating the final semester with my friends. A man, a boyfriend, a husband—none of those thoughts were in my head. I returned back to school and still stayed in contact with both TheNextDoorNeighbor and TheOneYourFamily-WantsYouToMarry. I'm not going to lie, I liked the attention, and I also liked the options. A girl's gotta have options.

My birthday is in April, and I was finally going to be in town for the weekend to celebrate it. For my twenty-first birthday, I spent the weekend traveling to Minneapolis for the National Mock Trial Competition. I had one drink the night before at an Italian restaurant that didn't even ask to see my ID. It was a chocolate martini. Delicious, but just not the way most people bring in their first year of being able to legally drink, and the one time I actually wanted to be carded, I wasn't! What?

This year, I decided to make up for the lack of celebration the year prior. Along with celebrating, I wanted either TheNextDoorNeighbor or TheOne-YourFamilyWantsYouToMarry to help me celebrate. It was a test of whether they actually wanted to make the effort for a relationship or not. Would either of them be willing to fly or drive out to Chicago and celebrate with me?

My first choice was TheNextDoorNeighbor. He lived the closest and had a short four-ish-hour drive to the city. I figured it wouldn't be difficult for him to come compared   to TheOneYourFamilyWantsYouToMarry, who had to fly from states away. Convenience over actual interest won out on who I invited first. Don't ever make this a reason to be with someone. If he or she feels the same as you, they will go the extra mile. As I learned from this experiment.

TheNextDoorNeighbor was wishy-washy from the start. He was really busy with law school and didn't know if he would have the free time to drive out for a night. Run. He's not worth it. If he can't make the time for one night with you, just say goodbye. I promise.

I wasn't going to wait around for TheNext-DoorNeighbor to make a decision, and I figured he would flake out no matter what. Next. I asked TheOneYourFamilyWantsYouToMarry. His answer? No problem, I'll be there! Alright…again, I'm thinking my parents know much more than I do in this area. I was so excited for him to come and couldn't believe he would fly in from dental school, but TheNext-DoorNeighbor couldn't drive a short-ish distance from law school. I'm telling you, if they like you, they'll make the effort. Don't waste your time on the ones who won't make the effort. Because as you'll see, I did waste my time, and all I got from it were lessons learned.

I never told TheNextDoorNeighbor that I had invited TheOneYourFamilyWantsYouToMarry, too. If push came to shove and TheNextDoorNeighbor actually did want to come last-minute, then I would let him know. In the meantime, I was excited for TheOne-YourFamilyWantsYouToMarry to fly in for the weekend and stay with me. I couldn't wait for my friends to meet him, and for a good weekend. Plus, maybe we'd finally share a kiss on the lips. Since we took things real slow…

He met me at my dorm room with a huge smile on his face. I couldn't believe he was there! It all seemed surreal to me. We got ready real fast that night and headed out to meet my friends. They all joined us on the train to Wrigleyville to dance the night away. TheOneYourFamilyWantsYouToMarry fit right in with all my friends. They loved him, and would continue to bring him up as an example of who they thought I should be with into the future. I wasn't surprised at all. He could get along with anyone; it's what I liked about him.

On the dance floor that night, my friends stole several pics of the two of us, including a pic of our first kiss on the lips. *How crazy would it be if we ended up together and our first kiss was documented for the rest of our lives?* Those were the thoughts I had. This was the time of Facebook, but I never posted that photo. I made a copy of it and gave it to him, but it would remain a photo shared between the two of us. Something I think we should all make sure to do. It's important to keep some things private; not everything needs to be shared on social media.

It was one of the best birthday celebrations I've ever had. We all danced the night away and enjoyed some late-night tacos. There's just something about tacos at two in the morning. They just taste better.

We stayed together that night in my tiny little twin dorm room bed. I don't even know how we were able to fit. It was completely innocent, nothing but shared kisses on the lips. It was just nice.

The next day, we woke up early and headed out to reunite with some of his friends who lived just outside the city. They were meeting us for breakfast. As we waited for a table and his friends to arrive, I received a call from TheNextDoorNeighbor. I didn't answer it, nor did I care anymore. He didn't show, and TheOne-YourFamilyWantsYouToMarry did. It's true—actions really do speak louder than words.

I loved TheOneYourFamilyWantsYouToMarry's friends. In fact, I'm still friends on Facebook with them to this day. They welcomed me into their fun group quickly and we spent the whole brunch laughing and joking around. He introduced me with a huge smile on his face and seemed excited to be with me. It all seemed so good, yet there was still something missing.

I tried to shake the feeling as we took the train back to my dorm for him to collect his bag and head to the airport. There was something holding me back from really falling for him. I couldn't quite explain why I wasn't able to really see a future with him anymore. This guy had flown from states away to spend the weekend with me, and it was full of excitement and energy. Yet here I was, wondering if we were really meant to be. If I really wanted to marry this guy.

I thanked him for a great weekend and for making the trip out and helped get him a cab to the airport. I decided to ignore those strange feelings and chalk it up to my heart trying to protect itself from getting hurt again. He was such a great guy, and I wanted to see what would happen with him.

I later spoke with TheNextDoorNeighbor. He'd seen on social media that TheOneYourFamilyWants-YouToMarry had come to visit me for my birthday. It upset him. I told him that he had no reason to be upset since I had asked him first and he didn't make the effort to drive out. He claimed it wasn't fair since he was busy with school. It was what it was, and TheNext-DoorNeighbor and I didn't talk much the rest of the year. I was tired of his excuses and wanted to concentrate on guys who made the effort to see me. I actually didn't end up seeing either of those guys the rest of the year. Most of my time was spent working one of the two jobs I had and finishing up my classes.

I did still make an effort to talk with TheOneYour-FamilyWantsYouToMarry. As the school year came to an end, I bought him a Chicago Cubs shirt and mailed it to him. He loved it and wore it a lot before we met up that summer. He and his family invited my family and me out to their lake house for a weekend of jet-skis and water-skiing.

Once again, we had a great weekend together, and our families got along so well. I could see us all doing this for years to come. Little did I know, it wouldn't work out that way. My feelings of uneasiness weren't nearly as strong as they had been after he met me in

Chicago. Then I met him out for drinks before he went to residency and I attended law school.

We met at a local restaurant in our home town. It was a conversation we needed to have before we both went our separate ways. Were we going to see what happened between the two of us or let it go? I really wanted to keep seeing where it went, but I also knew I would be starting school where TheNextDoor-Neighbor was also a student. Then he dropped this statement on me: "Ashley, I'm not getting any younger, and I'm looking for my wife. I want to find someone to marry."

Yes. A bomb. As I've said before, I'm pretty bad at hiding my emotions and I'm pretty sure my already large eyes still managed to grow two more sizes. I think I stopped breathing for a second, too. Most women would probably be excited for a successful guy like TheOneYourFamilyWantsYouToMarry to say such words to them. I, on the other, hand started to freak out. I was just about to start three years of school, and wedding bells were not in my thoughts for the near future. Plus, I felt like I barely knew TheOneYour-FamilyWantsYouToMarry. Sure, we'd shared several weekends together, but we didn't really spend them alone.

Similar to my experience with Mr. TooMuch-TooSoon, I panicked. I wasn't ready for such words from anyone at that point in my life. My goal was to become an attorney, not a wife. I wanted to get married, but it wasn't at the forefront of my mind. I wasn't quite ready, and clearly I wasn't ready for that with TheOneYourFamilyWantsYouToMarry. I was honest with him, too. I told him I wasn't ready to say those things, yet. I was about to start law school, and that's where I needed to focus my attention.

It was the turning point for whatever future may have happened between us. I was willing to see what would happen in the future, but he was ready to start locking things down. We were on two different pages, and without saying it, we were going our separate ways.

We spent one last night together. He drove me to a nearby drive-in movie theater. It's an outdoor theater with film projected onto a large billboard. You parked your cars next to radios that played the movie audio for you. I hope these places never go out of business. It's a great summertime treat.

He brought a futon top and blankets and laid them on top of his car. We cuddled and enjoyed one last night together. It was a goodbye without either of us really knowing it. One last feeling of butterflies in our hearts. One last kiss. We didn't truly believe it was the end when we parted ways that night, but we both had different plans for the future, and time would soon show us it just wasn't meant to be.

4 | Grad School

(You Better Find Someone)

My parents lived a short distance from where I attended law school and they graciously loaded up their van to drive my stuff to my new home for the next three years. We hit a pothole on the way in the middle of the night and ended up having to unload everything to get to the spare tire hidden under the bottom of my parent's mini-van. Not the greatest way to start off grad school, but also not the worst. Just one more bump in the road, similar to the many in my dating life.

TheNextDoorNeighbor

I went into the school year eager to hit the books and obtain my doctorate. I wanted to be successful, finish at the top of my class, and work in criminal law. There were no thoughts of meeting someone to date and potentially marry. It wasn't my goal, nor my focus. Again, I just assumed it would happen when it happened. The guy would just be "around," and we would click and start dating. Plus, TheNextDoorNeighbor went to the same school, and there was still unfinished business with him. Who knew what my love life would become?

At this point in a lot of my friends' lives, they were concerned with finding someone, getting married, and settling down. Apparently, at some point in time, society tells us once we finish school, we should find someone to couple up with and settle down. Our time is running out, and it must be done sooner than later. If we don't, well, there must be something wrong. I was even told by a fellow law classmate that my chances of getting a divorce exponentially increase when I marry someone I meet after law school rather than during.

What? First of all, I'd love to know who decided to investigate such a statistic. Second, he unintentionally motivated me to purposely wait for after law school to find someone in order to prove him wrong. I think a better rule is you have an exponentially harder time finding someone after law school who doesn't have some sort of baggage. Now that's a rule that makes more sense to me. I also want to note that this individual was married. It's as if he wanted to shove it in my face that he would hopefully never have to worry about divorce since he had managed to find his wife before the impending law school graduation date.

You should know as I was writing this I did stop for a second to quickly look this individual up on Facebook. It looks as if he is indeed still married and not divorced. Perhaps he needed the reassurance from such a statistic to assure him his marriage wouldn't fail. Apparently it worked. Good for him. You should all know, though, saying these types of things to single people is not helpful. In fact, I'd say it's a bit self-righteous. A way to let single people know they're doing it wrong and need to "fix" or "solve" their being single problem sooner than later.

Those of us who are single and looking for someone to date are trying to find someone. We're just not willing to settle or quickly find someone based on some dumb statistic or the fact we're getting older. Life is short, and if we're going to enjoy it, then we want to do it with someone who complements our lifestyle and helps us have more happy days than sad ones. If that takes time, then so be it. In the meantime, we're killing this enjoyment of life thing. Stop being jelly.

The first day of law school brought anxiety, the introduction of new friends, and new potential men to date. Unfortunately, most of the guys in my class were already dating or married. I don't think any of them would have been good for me either. We were just very different people. Plus, I was very distracted by TheNextDoorNeighbor being back in my life and seeing him pretty much every day in school. The law school was all in one building, and the total population of the school was around 300 people. You were bound to run into anyone.

It's hard to forget old feelings for someone. It's why I typically never stay friends with exes. No matter how much time has passed, there are usually still some feelings that can rear their ugly heads. It's not worth it to have the temptation of an ex around to possibly stir them back up.

In this instance, both TheNextDoorNeighbor and I were single, and both of us could feel those feelings of attraction slowly swirling around in the way we smiled at each other and interacted. There was no way we were going to get through the school year without something happening between the two of us. It didn't take long at all; it was just too convenient for us.

We didn't have to start from scratch. We already knew each other. It's the comfortability that causes so many people to go back with exes, to return home and reignite with an old flame. They know you. It's a blessing and a curse. There's something to say for meeting a new person and slowly figuring one another out. There's also something to say for not wasting a month or two trying to figure out a person and learning you're not right together instead of moving forward with someone you've already figured it out with.

TheNextDoorNeighbor and I had a lot in common with each other compared to others at the school. We both had dads who graduated from the same law school we were attending. We both loved international travel and studies, and we were both from a small city nearby. The thing is, if you try hard enough you can find connections with anyone. It's one of the hardest things about dating. Oh, you both enjoy watching *The Office*? You should date! There's something to say about finding something much deeper than your initial associations with each other.

Before school started, TheNextDoorNeighbor and his fellow unit neighbors of an old house decided to throw a welcome back to school party. I was one of the few first years to be invited. (That's what you call each class: first year, second year, third year. Super creative, I know…) I was excited to go and meet new people, but I was more excited to hang out with TheNextDoorNeighbor and see what happened.

The party was a lot of fun, a typical porch party with beer pong and music. It's what you do when you don't have a lot going on in your town. We had two bars in town and both had interesting vibes. There were only a couple local restaurants and literally two fast food chains, Subway and McDonald's. I was told when McDonald's opened for the first time, which had only been a couple years prior, there was a line down the street to order. A line. For McDonald's. I was definitely no longer in Chicago, and I would soon really wish I still was.

I quickly made friends with some other people from my class and managed to talk one of the girls into accompanying me to this party. I didn't want to show up alone, especially when TheNextDoorNeighbor and his friends all knew each other already. I waited for a bit after the party started, too. I didn't want to be the first one there. I texted TheNextDoorNeighbor that my friend and I were on our way and made the short walk to his porch party.

Pretty much every place in that town was walkable. It was one of the only good things about living there. I didn't have to worry about driving and it was super safe, so I could get drinks and walk home easily. I was nervous getting ready for the party. I didn't know what to expect and I still wasn't sure where TheNextDoorNeighbor and I stood. Did he like me? Did he want to date me? It would be how I felt for most of the time I dated him—unsure. Unsure about him and how he truly felt about me and whether we actually had a future together. Definitely a red flag, ladies and gentleman: you never want to be in a relationship with someone who continues to leave you guessing where you are with each other.

As I approached the house with my friend, the party was already in full swing. There were a ton of people, most of whom I had never seen before. I looked for the familiar face of TheNextDoorNeighbor. He knew I was on my way and he was nowhere in sight. I was hoping he'd be there to welcome me to the party and introduce me and my friend to the other people there.

He was not there to do that. Again, another sign that I should've walked away and never pursued anything with him.

It's true, though—there's something to say for a little challenge in relationships. You want it to be easy, but you also want it to be unpredictable. I chalked these interactions up to just a new exciting relationship, instead of recognizing it as incompatibility. (It's amazing how well you can convince yourself of such things).

Eventually he came out from inside his apartment. He did welcome me with an awkward hug, as if to try as hard as he could to hide any hint of us being attracted to each other from everyone else. That's what he truly cared about—what everyone else was thinking about him. It didn't matter what I felt about him or us; it only mattered what others would think.

The night was really just awkward. My friend and I stayed around and met new people, but towards the end of the night, we left to meet up with other classmates. I spent more time hanging out with other people than I did talking with TheNextDoorNeighbor. Yet, for some reason, I still wanted to date him.

We hung out here and there throughout the school year. There was never a lot of discussion on whether we were dating or not. We never told anyone about our relationship, not even our families. I decided to see what would happen and go with the flow, but per usual, I didn't let it get in the way of my life.

I joined several committees and groups in law school, including the Icelandic Exchange Program. It was a group on campus that hosted law students from Iceland for a few days during Halloween. The Icelanders loved celebrating Halloween because they didn't do it in their country. Then after hosting, and depending on funding, several members of the group would be chosen to take a trip to Iceland to stay with those same students. There was no guarantee who would be allowed to go on the trip, but hosting an Icelandic student increased your chance of being selected. I loved traveling, so I jumped on the opportunity to not only meet international people, but go and visit them in their home country. Who knew such a small town in rural Ohio would have such a program?

TheNextDoorNeighbor also enjoyed traveling and was studying in the International Law program at the same time he was working on his law degree. It was one thing we had in common. We enjoyed learning about different countries and being around international students. I met several of them studying in the program, and this group was another way to do that. For whatever reason, TheNextDoorNeighbor was not part of this group on campus. It didn't bother me, though.

I think it's important to do your own thing when you're in a relationship. Otherwise, there's a chance you lose a little bit of yourself. It's healthy to have your own interests and enjoy life to make sure you both enjoy life together without it becoming too mundane.

The other reason I feel this way has been seen as a bit morbid by some. Personally, I call it being realistic about life. The truth is, every day we spend alive is a blessing. No one truly knows what the future holds. One day, despite everything we try to do, we will lose someone close to us. We may lose a significant other, a friend, a parent, or a child. It's important to make and maintain your friendships and relationships with loved ones. They will be the ones to help you get through it. They will be your rock through those hard times, and you can be the same for someone else. If you fail to nourish those relationships, those people may not be around for you as much as they would've been otherwise.

So, with my morbid thoughts and genuine desire to meet Icelandic people and travel to their country, I joined the Icelandic Exchange Program. In October of that year, I hosted a blonde law student who had previously lived in California. Her English was perfect and she was really caring and kind. We got along right away and have remained connected through Facebook ever since. (One of the good things about social media—keeping you connected with people around the world.)

Her, along with about ten other Icelandic law students, traveled across the world to come and stay in middle-of-nowhere Ohio. (Don't worry, they also made time to stop in New York City along the way). All of us there had the same concern. Why would they want to travel all the way to the United States and come stay with us in *rural Ohio*? Would they enjoy it? Answer: they loved it. They wanted to visit us to see how most of America truly lives. They wanted to experience it. It's so interesting what foreigners find exciting about our country. It makes you appreciate your small town life a little more, too.

A group went to pick them up at the airport and drive them the hour and a half to our small town. We then linked up with our guests and brought them back to our apartments to stay for the next couple of days. Over the next few days, we took the students to a shooting range and Walmart for costume shopping.

Really, it's what most of the world thinks of America: guns and Walmart. They enjoyed it, especially the guys.

They all selected costumes, too, ranging from a nurse to a whoopee cushion. I decided to create my own costume that year. I cut out cardboard into the shape of nightstand and wore a lampshade on my head with a bright yellow for-sale sign that read, "For Sale: One Night Stand." I wish I could say I thought of the pun on my own, but I diligently searched for a creative but funny costume online and have to credit the idea to someone else. We all went out that night to other apartments in the area because, again, that's what you do in a small town without a lot of bars to choose from.

I had one of the most fun nights of my life. Even if you grew up in different countries and speak different languages, cheersing drinks with friends is the same in every country. Celebrating friendship and memories is always the same. It's one of the reasons I learn what the word "cheers" is in every country I visit. In Icelandic, it's *skál*. We spent all night raising our glasses as we crowded in an old, dark, dirty local bar. The carpets hadn't been replaced in years and the bathrooms left much to be desired. But none of that mattered; it was the people that created an atmosphere of richness and excitement.

There were several men in the group and all of them were super cute. There's something about being foreign that automatically increases any guy's attractiveness for me—an exotic mystique that draws me in with an instant appeal. They were all really kind, too, and interested in learning more about me and America. It was fresh, new, and exciting.

The time flew by with the students, and soon they were packing up to make a quick stop in N.Y.C. before heading back to Iceland. I would have dated any of the guys visiting, but it's kind of hard to do so when you live halfway across the world from each other. Surprisingly, you always hear stories of those couples who met on a plane ride or a cruise ship. There was an instant connection, and despite living so far from each other, they made it work. I enjoy listening to those stories, but I have a really hard time understanding how they work. I've never been able to make such a strong connection with someone in such a short amount of time. Sometimes I feel like I've made the connection, and it's magical, but it never lasts once I return home. I have never been able to understand the couples who have lasted.

It's also because of those couples and their stories that, as a single person, you will be constantly reminded of them. You'll be told every time you go on vacation or join a new group, "You never know who you're going to meet," or "Your new man could be in that group." First, we're already thinking that. It's crossed our mind, and we're secretly hoping the same thing happens for us. Second, stop. Don't say those things to us and remind us of your distant relative or friend who happened by chance to meet their-long lost lover on a red eye from Las Vegas.

Sure, tell us the stories as we join you for a night out or catch up over dinner. But don't bring it back up right before we leave on an exotic vacation or work conference. We're already thinking it, and you saying it out loud just puts more pressure on us. It causes us to wonder as we board the flight whether the cute guy sitting two rows over in the waiting area might end up sitting next to us on the plane. How we might strike up a conversation, and then the next thing we know we're getting married.

It sets this pretense on our whole trip. With every conversation we have with a stranger, there's a small voice in the back of our heads asking ourselves whether he could be the one. Then after an amazing time traveling, we return with this feeling of disappointment because we don't have a story to tell you about how we met this great guy. When, really, we had an amazing trip and would rather celebrate the good memories instead of the fairytale dream that never came true.

These thoughts joined me as I was accepted to travel to Iceland and stay with the Icelandic students. Would I meet someone? Would one of the guys I had met earlier suddenly profess his undying love for me? I also was excited to visit a new country and see how things differed from living in the U.S., all the while keeping an eye out for a potential future lover.

Iceland is beautiful. If you've never visited, I highly recommend you book your ticket and go. The people are very welcoming, and most millennials speak English fluently. I'm seriously impressed with those who can speak more than one language and do it so well.

For anyone out there making fun of someone tripping up on words or pronunciation of those speaking a second language, I encourage you to try it. It's hard. Instead of denigrating them, embrace and help them. The more we can communicate with each other, the better the world will be. The one thing I've learned in my travels is that no matter where you go or who you meet, we all want to live better lives and make better lives for our family and friends. In reality, we all speak the same language, just in different dialects.

We arrived in Iceland to snow and ice, pretty much fitting for a country with such a name. The Icelandic law students picked us all up at the airport in ReykjavÍk and drove us to their respective apartments to sleep for the night. The next day, we toured the U.S. embassy, Icelandic Supreme Court, and Icelandic prison. The prison was the most interesting. None of the prison guards carried guns, only tasers. All of the prisoners were able to attend school and work to earn money. They could use the money to purchase TVs and game consoles for their cells. Also, if they were well behaved and completed a good portion of their sentence, they were permitted to leave the prison for a full day and go wherever they wanted. The prison system was created with the intention of rehabilitating individuals instead of punishing them. They said the recidivism rate was low, meaning most people, after completing their sentences, would return to society and never commit a crime again. It seems the system was working for them. It would certainly take some time to integrate such a system in America's prisons, but perhaps it eventually would work the same.

After our legal and political immersion, we traveled out to the countryside to all stay together in a cabin with a hot tub. I really think the hot tub makes all the difference when staying in a cabin. It's so nice to have when it's freezing outside and you want a relaxing thing to do before passing out for the night. We partook in some Icelandic local beer, blood sausage, and this terrible liquor called Opal, which tasted like black licorice. I can still taste it now. Not my favorite. Not at all.

After a long day of tours, we relaxed and as the night got later, we all jumped in the hot tub. We were in the middle-of-nowhere Iceland, and there was little-to-no light pollution. All of a sudden, we looked up and the greenish-yellow glow of the northern lights was shining just enough for us to see them. We hadn't expected it or planned to see them, and sometimes that's exactly when things happen. Not always in dating, but definitely in adventures. It was by far one of the most beautiful things I've seen in nature. It's also something I want to experience again. I highly recommend traveling to experience such things in your life, too.

We went out the last night of our trip, and I met a lot of Icelandic men. One wrote his telephone number on my hand. Later I discovered it was missing a number. It just wasn't meant to be.

There wasn't a Mr. Iceland. I traveled, I explored, I met a ton of a new people, but still no Mr. Iceland. That's okay, too. Sometimes even when you push your boundaries, meet new people, and travel to new places, you still don't meet anyone. When single people are told they should put themselves out there more and experience new things where we could meet new people. We think about these moments. We want to tell you how we have put ourselves out there and pushed boundaries—sometimes much further than the person giving the advice. We bite our tongues, force smiles and thank-yous for your advice, all the while screaming inside to tell you our stories.

I had a trip many in their lifetime will never be able to experience. I'm grateful I had the opportunity and I enjoyed every moment. I write this section for those out there who continue to pressure their single friends and relatives. Everyone is different, and every path to love is different. Respect each other's paths and allow those who are still single to enjoy life and vacations without always having to wonder if they'll finally find a special someone to share their lives with. I'm living proof you can enjoy life even when you don't have someone to share it with at the moment.

The Texan

I wrapped up the rest of the first year of grad school, interacting with TheNextDoorNeighbor here and there. I still liked him a lot, but I was more focused on having a successful school year. I still had no idea where I stood with him. He treated me like an acquaintance when we hung out around other students at our school. It didn't stop me from wishing he wanted me more and hoping things would change. At the same time, it also didn't stop me from pursuing my interests and finding a way to study abroad that summer without him.

My Spanish-speaking skills have always remained subpar. In hopes of improving them and also traveling to a new continent, I applied for a study-abroad program in Santiago, Chile. It was also one of the few programs with an internship component that didn't require you to be fluent. I'd later learn fluency would have made my experience a little easier, but I was up for the challenge! I packed my suitcases up and flew down to Santiago, where I would experience a few more months of winter. The weather was probably my only regret of the whole trip. I don't know many people who enjoy having winter year-round. I am definitely not one of them.

I landed in the Santiago airport and searched for my ride and other members of my group. I quickly found them and piled into a large minivan with other random American strangers who I would soon be bonded with for life from our experiences. We all quickly introduced ourselves as the van drove us into the city and dropped us off at the school where we'd be taking classes for the summer. Luckily, the classes were all taught by American law professors. I was definitely not able to translate law classes from Spanish to English. They were hard enough to learn from in English.

This is where I met TheTexan. As you can tell by his name, he's from Texas. The program I attended was made up of students from Texas, Boston, California, and then me from Ohio. I'd never dated or really met many men from Texas. I truly believed they liked things bigger, and I fit the midwestern Ohio girl stereotypes much more than the big-hair, big-makeup qualities used to describe the women down south. Somehow, we hit it off anyway.

There was something that drew me to him and him to me. I can't quite put my finger on it, but every time we'd go out to the local bars, we would end up close together.

He was dark haired, dark featured, and well over six feet tall. He was handsome in a dorky kind of way. Not your typical prince charming, but charming in an awkward kind of way. Most importantly, he was kind and caring. You can always tell the truth about someone if you pay attention to how they act towards others, especially those they don't know. Does he hold the door open for a stranger? Does he thank the waitress for her kindness? I wouldn't write men off all together if this didn't happen, but these actions certainly increase my attraction.

We got along really well, and it was easy to talk to him, laugh with him, and let the night get away from us. I told him I liked him and wanted to see what would happen between us even though the program was scheduled to end in two and a half months. I mean, as much as I hate to admit it, it's true. You just never know who you'll meet, when you'll meet, or what your futures will hold. If all the other couples had it happen, why couldn't happen for me?

All was going great, and most everyone in the group saw that we were somewhat together and liked each other. Then—*record scratch)*—it all was shaken up by one person. Once again, another woman wanted to interfere in my happiness. She didn't care that he and I had been spending time together. All she cared about was herself, winning him over, and getting him away from me. I'm going to call her Miss TwoName.

See, Miss TwoName was one of those people who had two names for their first name. I have nothing against people who have two names for their first name; it's just that she would be really offended if you only used one of them. Sometimes, it takes extra breath to get the additional syllables out, and when you're from a town where no one has two names as their first, it's hard to get used to. Also, when you get mad to an extreme at people for only using one of your two names, it really just makes people want to do it more. Just saying.

This girl would sneak up to TheTexan every time I left for the bathroom or to re-fill my drink. She put her hands all over him and did anything and everything to try and get his attention. I am not this type of woman. I want to be with a man who sees me for who I am, who wants to be with me for those qualities and not because I'm throwing myself all over him. After a few times of seeing her do this, I walked straight up to him and told him exactly where I stood. I told him I liked him and wanted to see what would happen between us. I knew the program was only for the summer and I wasn't looking for him to be exclusive with me, but I also wasn't going to continue to see what happen if he was going to see Miss TwoName, too. Now, to be fair to him, neither he nor I was probably in the best state of mind to be having such a conversation, but I needed him to know. I then left. That's right, I left. I left knowing Miss TwoName was still at the bar and would most likely continue to throw herself on him. I figured if he felt the same way, he would make the right decision.

The next day, I found out, sometimes it does work out. If you choose the right guy and he wants to be with you, he will do the right thing. I was walking to school with my roommates, and one of them had been texting one of the roommates of Miss TwoName. See, she had continued to throw herself at him the rest of the night, just as I thought she would. In fact, she begged for him to come home with her. After her badgering, he gave in and took a taxi back to her apartment with her.

Then the story got good. She led him back to her room and immediately stripped naked. Again, this girl was willing to give him anything and everything without receiving anything in return. It's the type of girl I thought would always win with men. She didn't win, though. TheTexan left his clothes on and asked her, "I wonder if Ashley got home safe?" He then proceeded to pass out with his clothes on and didn't hook up with her. How do I know, you ask? Because apparently she continued to shout at her roommates during the ride to class the next morning, "How can a guy not do anything when he has a naked girl in bed with him? How?"

How, ladies? Because he liked me not her. Sometimes sticking up for yourself and what you want pays off. The girl who throws herself at a guy doesn't always win out, and even if she does that night, it's usually not for the long term. So trust yourself and trust him. If he's one of those good ones who truly likes you, it will work out in the end.

TheBrazilianFighterPilot

I stayed friends with TheTexan the rest of the trip, but it was never really the same after that night. I focused on enjoying the rest of the trip and keeping my distance from Miss TwoName. The rest of my time was filled with tons of trips, from wine tasting at a vineyard, white-water rafting on a river, to tours of a Pinochet torture camp. So many adventures and lessons on historical events. The trip flew by, and soon we were coming up on our last couple weeks in the country.

Several of us decided to sign up for a Santiago bar crawl. That's right, bar crawls are a thing all around the world. I had no expectations going into the night except to have one last fun night out. The first bar we came to was small in size and dimly-lit, a typical low-key neighborhood bar similar to those in the States.

I was with several other girls from my study program. Two of them were my roommates. It was in some way a final goodbye to our good times in the country. We grabbed some local beers and gathered around a cheaply made table on old wooden chairs. It had only been a few minutes before a group of guys sat at a table nearby.

They were loud and really cute. Shortly after they arrived, they eyed our table and started talking with us. There was one guy in particular who caught my attention. For the purposes of this book, I'll call him, TheBrazilianFighterPilot. As you can tell from the name, he flew planes for the Brazilian military. In fact, the whole table was filled with members of the Brazilian military. They were young, fit, and spoke English. All of them wore their military dog tags around their necks and were out to have a good time.

There was something about TheBrazilianFighterPilot. It was an instant attraction and connection. I wasn't even planning on meeting someone that night. It was just like all the other people I knew who met someone randomly. It all happened so fast and easily that I didn't trust it at first. I questioned his dog tags and fighter pilot status. In my head it all seemed made up. It had to be a pickup line, right? Then he pulled out his phone and showed me a picture of him in his green flight suit standing in front of a military plane. My guard was quickly falling down, I figured not many people would go to that length to pretend they were a military fighter pilot.

We laughed and talked about where we were from in our respective countries and what we were doing in Chile. He was there on holiday with his other military comrades. As we talked we continued to drink the free beer on the crawl and move closer and closer to each other, both of us with huge smiles on our faces. Soon it felt like we were the only two in the bar that night and no one else mattered. We wrapped up the first bar with an intimate kiss—we couldn't hold back any longer—and we had had plenty of liquid courage to help us.

As we got up to travel as a group to the next bar, he grabbed my hand. I noticed how much taller he was than me and just bigger over all. He was handsome, with a thick head of sandy brown hair and big brown eyes. Despite his large stature, I didn't feel threatened. He had a kindness about him and created a protective shield for me as we walked. I felt instantly safe and happy.

Who was this woman walking with a stranger, feeling so romantic? This was so unlike me. It was very rare for me to fall for someone so quickly. I started to understand what so many of my friends had talked to me about. The feeling you can't explain and you don't fully understand.

The next bar had a dance floor. A new chance to get even closer to TheBrazilianFighterPilot. He led me straight to the dance floor and pulled me close. We swayed together to the music as he took a hold of me and rocked my body from side to side along with the beat of the song. Soon, he swept me off my feet, literally. He grabbed me under my legs and he cradled me in his arms as we shared another intimate kiss. My friends from the study abroad program snapped a photo of that moment. I still have the photo to this day. Again, the moment was surreal.

We could barely stop kissing each other as we danced away the night and walked to the final bar. Another dance floor was in this one, too. It was getting close to the night being over. We were in the corner talking and kissing when he asked me to come home with him. In that moment I had two people in my head, one telling me, "Run! He's a complete stranger!" the other telling me, "Go! Trust the process!" I'm not sure to this day which answer would've been the best, but I went with the first voice.

Stranger-danger was a lesson I'd been given repeatedly growing up. Plus, this was the era after Natalee Holloway never returned from the Caribbean. I left, figuring if it was meant to be, then we'd find a way to reunite another time. I kissed him goodbye and squeezed him tight, promising to talk with him soon. Plus, I wanted my beer buzz to wear off to make sure this was real and not just an intoxicated infatuation. I grabbed a cab home and fell asleep yearning for more time with him, wondering if I would ever see him again.

He added me on Facebook, but we never really chatted. It was a one-night love story. One of those moments when many people continue their lives together, and one day a friend stands up at their wedding reception and tells the story. They talk about "love at first sight" and knowing the moment they met each other. I listen to those stories and think of these moments. How I completely understand how they felt.

I don't disagree with the realness of those feelings, or the fact people can truly feel in love with someone the first time they met. However, I think that feeling can be felt and the love story doesn't continue beyond that first meeting with someone. Some will say I'm wrong. The feeling I felt that day wasn't true love because it didn't continue. This is another lesson for those couples out there who have only felt that one moment with the one person they ended up being with for life.

Trust your single friends when they tell you they've felt it, too. When it ends, it's painful. Obviously, it's more painful when we're with those people for longer than a single day, but it still stings a little. You get a taste of something amazing, you being to understand what your coupled up friends have and you want more of it. But there's no love store to go to and get your fill. We can't convince someone to stay with us and fight for us. We just have to keep putting ourselves out there and hope that one day, when we have that feeling again, it actually sticks, all the while hoping the other person doesn't break your heart one more time.

TheNextDoorNeighbor

They say you never know who you'll meet when you travel or change up your routine. It's true; those people are not wrong. I met two amazing guys on my trip. Neither of them became anything serious, but I learned a little bit more about myself and what I wanted in a partner. I also learned what I didn't want in a partner. I returned back to school with a renewed since of self and staying true to what I wanted. However, there were still feelings for one guy I couldn't quite push away. TheNextDoorNeighbor still had a hold on me.

He had spent the summer in Washington, D.C. working in an internship program and stayed in the Georgetown dorm rooms. When I got home, we swapped photos of our trips. He had also bought an old wood-paneled Wagoneer and drove it home. In a lot of his pictures was a woman he said was just a friend. I trusted his answer, but not fully.

The summer was over just as quickly as it started and we were soon returning to school. I had earned a position on an international moot court team called Jessup. It's basically an oral argument team where we wrote arguments and competed in oral arguments in Chicago during the second half of the year. TheNextDoorNeighbor was my coach. I was excited about it because it meant we would be spending a lot of time together. However, he used it as an excuse for why we couldn't tell anyone about our relationship.

That's right—we finally solidified our relationship as an exclusive one and started to spend more time together. But since he was my coach, he didn't want people to think he was treating me any differently, and he didn't want anyone in our business. So we didn't tell anyone.

I half-heartedly agreed with him. I had grown up in a small school, our grad school had fewer than three-hundred people total, and everybody knew everybody. There was a part of me that wanted to keep the relationship quiet and keep others out of it. It made it a little more exciting. Then there was another part of me that hated it. It made me feel like he was ashamed to date me and didn't truly want to date me.

I'd learn from this secret love that I would never want to do it again. If you want to be with someone, it shouldn't matter what other people think or say about it. It's about you two, and you should want to let other people know how happy you are together. If you're not doing that, there's probably something wrong with the relationship. If I had accepted this red flag from the beginning, I would've saved myself a lot of heartbreak. Instead, I chalked it up to every relationship being different, that after school ended we would finally go public and all would work out okay. I'd later find out there was another reason he wanted to keep it so quiet.

We spent a ton of time together, and despite him not wanting to, he did treat me differently than my three other teammates. He was much harder on me. I thought maybe it was part of my imagination until one of my teammates asked me about it. I finally broke down and explained the situation. She was one of the only people at the school who knew about the relationship. He told me he was harder on me because he knew I could do better; really, I think he was overcompensating to make sure no one even had a hint of attraction between the two of us.

Looking back now, I fought with him a lot over the dumbest things. I didn't want to be around him anymore after the competition. He treated me so harshly, and I was tired of it and hiding our relationship not only from our classmates but our families. It didn't make sense to me anymore. He eventually came over to my apartment right before he graduated and told me he no longer wanted to date me. I cried, went back to my room, got his sweatshirt, and handed it back to him. I didn't want to see him or have anything of his in my room anymore. It hurt a lot. At those moments, you forget about all the fights and incompatibility. You think about all the fun times you enjoyed, and you don't want those to be gone forever.

We didn't talk for some time after that, but soon school was over and we were back at our houses, swimming in the lake and laughing. One night we took one of my family's canoes out. It was pitch-black out, with the glow of the bright full moon shining over us. I climbed to his end of the canoe and started to kiss him. Unfortunately, the canoe was not intended to hold that much wait at one end and we quickly found ourselves in the mucky water with algae hanging off our heads. I laughed so hard that night as I climbed to the side and he slowly dragged the canoe out of the water. It was those moments that made me fall for him again and wish we had more time together.

One day, he asked to bring a few of his classmates over to swim and take a break from studying for the bar exam. I agreed and couldn't wait to see him again. One of those friends was another blonde law student, someone I didn't hang out with much but always thought was a nice person. They swam and then packed up and headed out. TheNextDoorNeighbor stayed behind and we talked more, and kissed me again that night. Maybe we just needed a break from school to realize we had a good thing going.

Then I returned to school and found out he had hooked up with the blonde student he asked to have over. That was the final straw for me. I texted him and told him how disrespectful he was for bringing her over there and kissing me later that day. He tried to call and explain things, but I didn't want to talk to him. The fact that he brought her over to my family's house felt like a smack in the face. I no longer trusted him. I wish I could say I cut all ties at that point, but I didn't.

I continued to talk with him as I started my final year of school and he figured out what he was going to do by living with his parents. Soon, he moved to D.C. to find a job, and I sent him a care package filled with food and a tie for him to wear for job interviews because he hadn't brought any with him. He appreciated it a lot and wanted me to come visit him. I agreed, and I was excited to see what would happen between us. Maybe I'd been too quick to judge and he really was something special. I mean. We had spent so many years together in some capacity at this point. Then, right before I was going to book a flight out, he told me he didn't think it was a good idea.

He had started to date someone. Not just someone—the girl he had met the summer before while interning in D.C. In that moment, I realized he never really wanted to keep our relationship a secret from all our classmates and family. He wanted to keep it a secret from her. There's no way for me to prove it, but I know he was still communicating with her over the whole past year. He had told me we couldn't work out because I "didn't understand his music." This girl had gone to several concerts with him and I guess "understood" his music interests more than me.

The truth is, he just wanted to be with her more than me. I wasn't right for him, and she was. It wasn't because I didn't get his music, it was because we weren't right for each other. It was a hard pill to swallow. I did some major Facebook stalking of the both of them, each time hoping to see some evidence that their relationship had ended and it didn't work out for him. A part of me wanted him to hurt like he had hurt me. Then I finally unfriended him and unfollowed him. I let it all go because it didn't matter. My constant interest in his life was affecting my own life and not allowing me to move on and meet someone new.

He ended up marrying that girl years later. I can now say I'm happy for him and I wish him the very best. Eventually, you see that some things are not meant to be. You never forget about that person and what you shared with them, but you let them go. You start to realize that not all those days together were good ones and you try to look for someone with whom you have more good days than bad and a better connection.

Mr. I'mAChangedMan

It took time for me to get over TheNextDoorNeighbor, but it didn't stop other guys from pursuing me. The school year was soon coming to an end, and I had *almost* completely moved on from TheNextDoorNeighbor. Almost. Really, I still thought about him a lot, but I knew I didn't really have a chance with him. At the same time, I also wasn't fully ready to move on. Then Mr. I'mAChangedMan asked me on a date. I agreed, because why not? Grabbing food and a drink with someone is never that big of a deal.

Mr. I'mAChangedMan had a reputation in our school for being with a lot of girls. He flirted with a lot of students, including the ex-girlfriend of my soon-to-be male roommate. I didn't trust him and just figured I was one more girl he wanted to add to his list. I was willing to go out with him, but my guard was up. I agreed to go on a date with him, but I had every intention of asking him some follow-up questions on that date if it started to get serious.

He told me he would pick me up at my apartment at 5:00 on a Saturday night. I had spent most of the day in the library studying for one of my finals and decided to lay down for a nap. I was actually still in bed when I heard him knock on my door. I lifted my head in a state of "oh, crap." I had clearly overslept. I wiped the drool from the corner of my mouth and quickly got up. I took a quick look in the mirror, shrugged my shoulders, and opened the door.

He was wearing a black leather jacket, smelled of some good (but a little strong) cologne, and had clearly just had his hair cut. He asked if I was ready, to which I responded, "Yup, I just need to grab my purse." I turned around inside really fast and grabbed my purse quickly, then followed him out to his car. It was the typical Toyota sedan. He opened my door for me (I gave him some points for that), and inside I could tell he had gone earlier to have it cleaned thoroughly. I mean, I think I would've eaten food off the floor if asked, it was that clean.

I was shocked. He clearly had put way more effort and thought into this date than I had. It made me think maybe he really had become a changed man. I let my guard down just a little bit. He then drove us to a nearby town for a nice dinner at an Irish pub.

I don't remember too much more of the night, but I do know he was a gentleman. Despite all of this, I had a hard time forgetting all of the rumors I had heard of him. When I asked him about them, he shrugged his shoulders and said he had changed. He didn't exactly disagree with them. For those reasons, along with the fact I wasn't over TheNextDoorNeighbor, I wasn't able to let him in. I didn't trust him.

See, after you've trusted people and they hurt you, you start to look for red flags you ignored in those past individuals. When you see them, you can't help but take those flags at their worth. Even if the person tells you and, in more of a superficial way, shows you he's changed, you don't fully believe him. It's like you need him to show you through another person first, then you'll believe him, or he'll need more time to really prove it's not a temporary change but a permanent one.

On top of my failure to fully believe he changed were my lingering feelings for TheNextDoorNeighbor. I wasn't fully over him, and Mr. I'mAChangedMan wasn't meeting the same standards that I had given to TheNextDoorNeighbor. I'm not really sure what happened next between us. I remember him walking me to my door and giving him a hug, but neither of us reached out after that night. I think we both knew the timing wasn't right between us. Plus, the summer was starting, and he was returning home to another state while I started my summer job in my small hometown in Ohio.

TheFriendWhoNeverKnewILikedHim

I had secured a job with the local prosecutor's office during my final year of law school and accepted a position as coach for the moot court team I had competed with the year before. This year was going to be busy, and I welcomed the distractions from thinking about TheNextDoorNeighbor. I had moved in with another woman and man from my class, and we shared a huge house on the main street of the town. We all shared a common love for criminal law and worked hard in school.

I had grown close with my female roommate during the end of the year before. I'm going to call her TheCrazyOne. Now, you may think I'm being a bit harsh by giving her that name. I'm telling you, I'm not. I also didn't realize she deserved such a name until well after I knew her. I should've realized it once she told me so many of her other girlfriends no longer wanted to be her friend and treated her poorly. Be very leery of people who claim all these people are mean and bashing them for no reason. There is always a reason.

I agreed to move in with her the next year because I missed having company in my apartment. Plus, the final year of law school wasn't supposed to be as difficult as the previous two years had been. I figured it would be a good time to have someone to hang out with and go out with to the only two bars in our small town. She seemed excited, too, and also proposed to add another person into the mix. She had also been talking with another friend of hers, TheFriendWho-NeverKnewILikedHim about living with us, too.

I didn't know him very well at the time. Of course, I knew who he was; the class sizes were so small, there was no way not to know everyone in your class. He invited TheCrazyOne and me over to the small rental he shared with an upperclassman who was graduating. We had all agreed to live together for our last year of law school, and TheFriend-WhoNeverKnewILiked-Him thought it would be ideal for TheCrazyOne and me to move in with him. Into a place where only two people lived. Where two guys lived for the past two years.

TheCrazyOne and I toured the small mobile home with broken doors, dirty dishes in the sink, and a bathroom that looked like it hadn't been cleaned in quite some time, and definitively disagreed on wanting to move in to that location. We quickly started looking around and found a large house on a main street that was clean and allowed each of us to have our own room. I thought it was a good start to a new year. However, there is one detail I left out. TheCrazyOne had confided in me that she was crushing on TheFriendWhoNeverKnewILikedHim.

At the time, I had no feelings for him. In fact, I wouldn't develop feelings for him until after we graduated. So the issue I had with TheCrazyOne liking him wasn't due to jealousy. No, it was concern.

I was worried she would attempt to pursue him and he wouldn't reciprocate, and our living situation would become awkward. Or he would bring a girl back to the house and it would cause her to get angry. I talked with her about it, and she insisted I shouldn't worry. She was wrong. I definitely should've worried. It actually wasn't even for the reasons I thought. No, it was for jealousy. Only it was *her* jealousy of *me*.

The summer quickly passed, and soon we were all back in the small town and moving into our shared house. I took the bedroom upstairs and TheCrazyOne and TheFriendWhoNever-KnewILikedHim took the two bedrooms downstairs. I figured if anything were to happen, I could just hide away upstairs in my room. Not my worst idea.

As the school year got into full swing, so did football season. TheFriendWhoNeverKnewILikedHim rooted for the same college football team as I did even though neither of us went to the school. We were raised to be passionate Buckeye fans through and through. Each weekend, we would order pizza or grab snacks and some beer and sit on the couch to watch the game together with TheFriendWhoNever-KnewILikedHim's dog named, you guessed it, Buckeye. I thought nothing of it and loved having a fellow fan join me as I watched. We cheered on the team through the TV and high-fived each other after each touchdown. It was fun camaraderie, and it irritated TheCrazyOne.

Being from Pennsylvania, TheCrazyOne was not a die-hard Ohio State fan and started to seem annoyed TheFriendWhoNeverKnewILikedHim and I were hanging out more to watch the games. It was completely platonic, and we asked her to join us every time. She declined and instead spent her time in the library. Listen, I was in the library a lot, too, but there comes a time when you need to take a break. Sometimes, too much studying does you a disservice.

Along with the games, we would sometimes come home after studying and working (we both had litigation internships) after a long week and decide to rest and watch a movie on Friday nights. It was never a planned event. We would both be home and exhausted and just want to sit on the couch. We didn't even sit on the same couch. He was on one and I was on mine on the complete opposite side of the room. Again, it was anything but romantic.

TheCrazyOne didn't work and just spent her time in the library. She would come back later than us and see the scene in the living room. We'd both say hi to her and welcome her to join us. She was always annoyed and always declined our offers. What can you do? You can't force someone to have a good time with you. We just left her alone.

I grew closer and closer to TheFriendWhoNever-KnewILikedHim over the year, but it was never in a romantic way. I really saw him as if he were my brother. He always nagged at me and ate my favorite food in the house. He would always buy healthy food and indulge in my snacks. If it was just a little bit, I wouldn't be as bothered by it, but he would eat the whole box of whatever I bought. Not cool.

A lot of the girls in our class seemed to like him and flirt with him a lot. I never understood why. He was a nice guy and worked hard, but he could be so annoying. Plus, I was still not fully over TheNextDoorNeighbor. I spent most of this year digging into work, school, and preparing to sit for the bar exam. I knew I wasn't ready for a new relationship. I was still healing from my recently broken heart.

It's important to take time to yourself after a breakup with someone. You need the time to restart and allow yourself to open up again to someone new. Otherwise, you spend a lot of your time comparing each new guy you meet to the connection you developed with your past significant other. They will never match up and you'll end up feeling defeated, often times hurting other people who are ready for a relationship.

Also, everyone takes a different amount of time to heal after the end of a relationship, no matter how long or short it is or how long people tell you it should take. Pay attention to your own thoughts and feelings and don't listen to others. You'll know you're finally ready to date again when you go to a party and don't think about your ex during it, even more so when you start thinking about someone new. It takes however long you need it to take.

During this year, TheFriendWhoNeverKnewILiked-Him brought different girls over and talked with me about his girl issues. He talked with me about my guy issues, too, but it was really just me still trying to move on from TheNextDoorNeighbor. He was really supportive, though, reminding me of my worth and how I deserved a great guy. Later, when we talked, he would stop saying those things and just continue to ask the same question I ask myself: "Ashley, how are you still single? I just don't get it!" Yeah, TheFriendWho-NeverKnewILikedHim, I don't get it, either.

The school year quickly came to an end and we were soon spending every day with each other studying for the bar exam. Even at this moment, I still didn't have feelings for him. There were maybe cute little moments, but never a desire to pursue anything with him. He always did annoying things like driving with me for an hour and half to go take the bar exam, only to find out he had never reserved a hotel room. So he ended up sleeping on an air mattress on my hotel room floor. Still, he never annoyed me enough to not want to be his friend but enough for me to not want to date him.

We packed up and moved our stuff out of the home we had shared all year. Memories of late-night movies, football games, and house parties. It was a good time, but it was time for our new adventures. He was heading to work for the military, and I was heading to work in Columbus, Ohio for the State. We said our goodbyes but promised we'd see each other soon. Just like that, my many years of school had finally come to an end. With it came an end for a way to meet guys somewhat organically, get to know them, and potentially date them.

After this stage, dating began to get even harder. Besides work or joining an activity, club, or group in a city, there's no other way to really meet other people except through a dating app. It's during this stage of life that people who met their significant others in school truly don't understand why it can be so difficult for some people. They just happened to go to a college house party and met the man of their dreams.

What they forget is that there are no longer house parties in the adult world. There's no longer that comfortability that you can talk to anyone at the party because they somehow know someone else there. Now you're at public bars with complete strangers, most if not all of whom have spotty dating pasts that's left them with scars and baggage. It's dating apps filled with people exaggerating their descriptions and editing their photos. It's making it to the final level of the game and having all your obstacles doubled.

It's by no means what I would call a "fun time." It's time-consuming, tiring, defeating, and hard for so many people to understand who have never had to go through it. But more and more people are experiencing it every year. For those of you living it, I get it. You're not alone. For those of you who haven't, welcome to the world of online dating.

5|Adult Life

(Welcome To The World Of Online Dating)

I moved to the capital of Ohio after law school. It wasn't exactly where I wanted to be, but it was more of an environment I wanted to live in than the one I was in during law school. There were more single people my age and a downtown life with more than one or two bars. Unfortunately, I'd learn most people there hung out with groups of friends they already knew from high school or college. I didn't go to high school or college in any of the surrounding schools, so it was somewhat difficult to break into those groups, but I did my best.

My first job was with the State government, and I started with a group of around fifteen others from law schools around the country. It was a good start to my search for friends and men. However, as you grow older, the pool of men you meet isn't what it seems at first sight. Normally, when you're younger, the group is mostly single men with a couple in casual to semi-serious relationships. Once you reach mid-twenties, it's the opposite. The men are usually married or in a serious relationship with a few still available. About half of our group was married, some with kids on the way.

I also connected with an old friend from high school before moving to Columbus, and she introduced me to another blonde dancer-attorney who lived in the city. She thought it would be a good idea for us to meet and become roommates. I was excited to meet her and have another person in the city to show me around and introduce me to new people.

I jumped right into the city by signing up to volunteer at a local hospital and creating a dating profile on one of the dating apps. Years later, I will have used almost every dating app created. They're all mostly the same with only slight differences. You go on and connect to a social media platform to pull in some data like your name, age, school, and photos. Then you add as much or little detail about yourself that you want. You're asked about your interests, such as political party, workout type (daily or monthly), and the type of vacations you like to take. All of these things are supposed to help you match with a potential partner.

As a woman, it's really on you to weed out the good from the bad. I find that most men swipe right, (meaning they say yes to wanting to meet) on almost every woman in the app. They usually don't read your profile and usually only look at your first photo, so make sure it's a good one. I also firmly believe some of the apps create fake profiles of very attractive models who don't really have a profile. Maybe they just didn't swipe to connect with me, but I'm pretty confident they were created to lure women onto the app and use it under unrealistic and false pretenses.

I typically use the apps for short periods at a time. One month here, then a month to take a break from it. It's time-consuming and filled with all sorts of people. I was reprimanded for not responding on time or not having free time for them to meet me the next night. How they had six figure salaries and any woman would be lucky to date them, and I should make myself more available to meet up with them. After a while, you start to get cynical. Once I start feeling annoyed by having to respond to people on the app, I take a break. It's best for me and for any one I might talk with on the app.

I really suggest everyone take a break here and there while online dating. It's important to refresh and meet people when you're in a good place. I've even told guys on the app that they should probably take a break from it and restart once they're not so angry about previous women they had met on the app. It's even harder to deal with when your friends in relationships tell you how fun the apps must be. How they're jealous they haven't used them and want to see your phone and swipe for you.

People, people, people. This is your friend's *real* dating life. It's not some digital game they're playing for fun. It's exhausting, and sometimes super defeating. You treating it as some "fun game" is a bit demoralizing. On top of this, there are several people who are in relationships and decide to get on an app when they're feeling insecure and unhappy. They're not *actually* looking for a relationship, they're just seeking attention. If you're one of those people, please stop. You need to find love and support in your significant other, and if you don't feel satisfied from them, then I'd suggest ending it and getting on a dating app when you actually want a relationship. It's already hard enough for us single people, and you're just making it that much harder.

As I perused the different profiles, I quickly started going on dates with guys. Most of them were only one date and they were usually not good at all. There was HandsyPete, who tried to rub my leg on our second date to a movie. I should've known that's what he wanted to do in a dark movie theater. Then Mr. WeekendTrip wanted me to travel to Kentucky with him for a weekend after one date together. There was also Mr. Catfish, who went by a different name on his dating profile and said, "Well, a pretty girl like yourself" before he said anything to me on our three-hour coffee date.

These dates were turning into a second job for me. As much as I tried to change my strategy or give guys a second date to see if maybe I wasn't giving them a chance, it didn't work. I don't even have names for many of the dates. Some ended with neither of us texting each other, and with others, I was upfront and told them I wasn't interested. I really didn't (and still don't) have much luck on the dating apps. But I did meet several guys outside the dating apps.

TheOneYourFriendRecommends

There's something about a close friend introducing you to someone else. You automatically let your guard down a little more than you would for a complete stranger. Especially if you're close with the friend who introduces you. You trust their judgment and believe them when they say the other person is a good one and you should give them a chance. I've since learned to not always trust your friends. They also have no idea what they're doing when it comes to love. Give it a go, but don't let your guard down too much.

See, TheFriendWhoNeverKnewILikedHim was still just my friend at this point in my life. We would talk periodically about our lives, including who we were dating at the time. He had a good friend living in Columbus, too. I'm going to call him TheOneYour-FriendRecommends. I actually ran into TheOneYour-FriendRecommends at a bar after work one day and offered to buy him a drink. I found out he had recently broken up with his girlfriend of six years and felt bad for him. I truly wasn't looking to date him and genuinely felt bad for his situation. My kind gesture was apparently seen as more than just a gesture by TheOneYourFriendRecommends, and he called up TheFriendWhoNeverKnewILikedHim shortly after happy hour ended that night.

I was shopping in the grocery store after the bar that night when I got a call from TheFriendWhoNeverKnewILikedHim, recommending I date TheOneYourFriendRecommends. He told me how he's a great guy, really smart, and genuinely a good person. I told him I never really looked at him that way, but I wasn't opposed to going on a date with him. TheFriendWho-NeverKnewILikedHim sounded more excited than I did about this future date. I figured if TheFriendWho-NeverKnewILikedHim made such an effort to call me and recommend his friend, then he must be a good guy.

Soon I was on my first date with TheOneYourFriendRecommends. He picked me up and drove me to dinner. I don't really remember the first date we went on. It wasn't bad, but it was also nothing special to remember forever. We would then date for a couple more months. I met his childhood friends and we talked every day. It all seemed to be going well until one day, I picked him up to go try out a crepe dessert place downtown. I was excited to try something new with him, and it felt like we were finally getting to a point of exclusivity. Maybe he'd finally be the boyfriend I'd take home for the holidays.

Then, as we were driving back to my apartment to eat the delicious chocolate, strawberry, whipped cream-covered crepes, he said something I'll never forget. He said, "Ashley, you know I'm not a good guy."

We weren't even talking about anything particular when he said this to me. I was a bit caught off guard by this statement and confused why someone would say this to anyone. Looking back, he must've felt guilty about something he had done. I'll never truly know. After he made that statement, though, I assured him he was a good guy. I thought he was just looking for some compliments. But it would never be the same, and soon he stopped wanting to hangout altogether.

He eventually met someone else on a dating app and was no longer interested in me. I was really just a rebound to get him back on his feet after the demise of his six-year relationship. He ended up marrying that girl, the one right after me. In the end, I knew he wasn't right for me, and he really did teach me quite a few lessons about life and the dating world.

He taught me to always believe when a person says something to you. If they tell you they're a bad person, believe them. People don't just say those things to say them. Also, don't always trust your friend when they recommend someone for you. They may have your best interest in mind, but they don't actually know how two people will be when they're together. Accept it as an introduction, but don't read anymore into it. Lastly, make sure a person is ready to be in a relationship with you. This final lesson has been a hard one for me to learn.

There's usually no real way to know if someone is ready to date. Even when you ask the person, they may tell you they're ready, but they could not only be lying to you about that, but also lying to themselves. I guess my only advice here is that their actions tend to speak louder than their words. If they say they care about you but aren't showing you, then they may not be ready. Sometimes, you won't know until they finally start to pull away and eventually end it. It sucks, but at least they end it and don't drag you on for years. There's always a somewhat silver lining to every breakup.

Mr. LiarLiarPantsOnFire

After working for a year at my job, I decided to change it up and move to a new department. I was soon working in a new building on a new floor. Sometimes a change as small as changing departments in your company can open up doors to new relationships. Little did I know, this job would open up my world to a guy whose office door was just two down from mine.

I didn't meet him the first few months I was in the office. He was working on a short-term contract for a military base in another state. All I saw was his dark office and name plate. If only his name plate had read "Mr. LiarLiarPantsOnFire," maybe then I'd know to stay clear. Unfortunately, attraction for someone tends to blind you from seeing the truth until you've let your guard down and it's too late to protect yourself.

His first day back in the office, we crossed paths several times. You couldn't help but notice him. He was much younger than most of the other men in the office by more than a decade. He was also fit and wore nicely tailored suits. There was an instant attraction between us; we both felt it.

The moment he saw me, he stopped in his tracks and turned quickly around to introduce himself to me. He had big eyes and a bright white smile. I couldn't help but feel drawn to him. He introduced himself briefly to me and then took off to do work. As soon as he left, I made it a mission to find out more about him. I needed to know if he was single or not. If he was dating someone, well, it wouldn't be the first time; he'd be friend-zoned and not an option. But perhaps the timing was actually right this time and he was available.

I immediately started asking my friends in the office if they knew him and whether he was dating or in a relationship with anyone. Most didn't know much about him, and one of my friends tried to pry for me in a conversation with him, but he didn't let on about having a girlfriend. Not exactly the response I was looking for, but the unsure nature of answers combined with his frequent stops into my office to chat about what I can only assume were made up legal concerns to give him an excuse to talk with me was enough for me to think he was single and he liked me.

Soon, our work conversations were turning into personal conversations. He told me about his military service and his somewhat difficult family life growing up. The more we talked, the more I liked him. I wanted to find a way to see him outside of work. The opportunity soon became available when he invited me out to celebrate his birthday with some of his other friends in the office. I excitedly agreed and couldn't wait to see where the night would lead us.

My close friend happened to be joining us at the happy hour, too. I figured this was great because I would feel comfortable knowing more people there. I told her about Mr. LiarLiarPantsOnFire and how I thought he liked me and wanted to see where things would go with him tonight. She then told me she thought he had been flirting with her, but maybe he was just a flirty guy. I should've realized then that this guy was truly a flirt with almost every woman. I thought I was different because we had shared some personal stories with each other, but then I started to question if he might be doing that with everyone.

My game plan was quickly changing from finding a way for us to have alone time to finding out if he actually liked me at all or was just a huge flirt. Welcome to the dilemma of a single person. I actually found out later that there were a few men who apparently made efforts to flirt with me and I had no idea they were interested in me at all until they confessed to me years after the fact. Then you have the other side of the spectrum where the person is so outgoing and flirtatious with a lot of people that you're not sure whether you're receiving an innocent comment or being put on notice that he likes you. I really believe these people act this way to have a defense if you turn down their advances. They just say they weren't hitting on you, they were just being friendly. Really, they were hitting on you, but didn't want to admit it after you shut them down.

What I've learned from these situations is that it's better to just go up and see if someone would want to go on a date with you instead of playing these guessing games. However, it's a lot easier said than done. It's hard to work up the courage to ask a person out, especially if it's someone you see often or who is in your friend group. You never know how they're going to react, or if they turn you down, whether they'll be weird around you for weeks, months, or even years after. Once you feel that sense of embarrassment from a person rejecting you, it's hard to brush it off and try again with others. So, I get it. But, I still do believe it's better to just get it out in the open instead of hanging onto it, not knowing how the other person feels.

I wish I could say I went up to Mr. LiarLiarPantsOn-Fire and asked him if he'd like to go on a date with me. I didn't. Nope. Instead, I spent the night trying to see if he focused his attention on me or showed any interest in wanting to date me. How can you tell, you ask? I really just based it on whether he spent more time interacting with me during the night or whether he would look over at me if he was in a different area of the bar. You know, real scientific research.

It seemed like he kept trying to get my attention all night, but I've had guys in my past do that to me (see: Mr. Italiano) and we went nowhere, so I still wasn't fully sold. Then my friend started noticing it, too. She told me she thought I was right and that he did like me. That was the sign I was looking for.

I started to try and show him I was interested in him, too, by touching his back when I talked with him. Soon, people started to head home from the first bar, and only a few of us made our way to the next one. Mr. LiarLiarPantsOnFire and I were alone at the bar and sharing a kiss. It was a good kiss. It was a kiss of passion, and one that we both had been holding back for weeks.

Then, as we were wrapping up to head to our homes, I saw him texting a girl. He had been texting a lot that night, actually. I figured he was just responding to all his friends wishing him a happy birthday, but this particular girl had been messaging him a lot. I asked him about her. I asked if he was dating her. His answer? She was an ex of his. They had dated when he was working out of state and he had ended it with her when he left.

I believed him. *Why would he lie about that*, I thought? Plus, he said it casually and naturally. It made sense that he would've met someone when he was there working for several months and end it right before he left. I figured she still wasn't over him and he was being nice. I shrugged it off and gave him one last kiss before heading home for the night.

The next couple weeks at work were good, and we talked more. We started to go out together for drinks and food after work. I was really starting to like him and excited to see what would happen between the two of us. He seemed so caring and sweet. He made me feel comfortable, and I could talk to him about anything. Then, more and more people kept telling me he had a girlfriend.

I told them the same story he told me. "No, no. He *did* have a girlfriend, but they broke up when he moved back to Ohio." They all said they didn't think they were broken up. I didn't listen to them, mostly because I was happy and I didn't want it to be true. I trusted him.

Soon enough, a friend of Mr. LiarLiarPantsOnFire had friended me on social media. The friending allowed me to see his friends. Mr. LiarLiar-PantsOnFire's picture was one of the top profiles of suggested friends. His name on the social media platform was different enough that I would not have found him through normal searching. I clicked his profile, and my mouth dropped open. I couldn't believe it.

There it was, in a large photo above his profile picture. A giant photo of him and a girl. Not a sister or a mom. No, it was clearly a girlfriend. You know, him posed with both of his arms around her, both of them looking like they're in love with each other. I couldn't believe it. Everyone was right. He was a huge liar. He hadn't broken up with her. There she was in bright colors, staring out me from my phone screen.

I immediately took a screenshot and texted it to him. I didn't write anything. I just sent him that image. He didn't answer, because what could he really say at this point? I'd caught him red-handed. Thanks, social media.

Eventually, I confronted him and asked him if that was the girl he had told me about. He said that was her. I then asked if they really did break up. He admitted they were still together.

I was pissed. I walked out of the office that day without our usual goodbyes. I didn't want to talk to him or see him. Unfortunately, I decided to date someone whose office was in the same hallway as mine. People always tell you not to date people at work. Usually those people are in relationships and don't have to date and find someone else. You know the potential repercussions if you do date someone. You realize if it ends poorly, you'll still have to see them. But you tell yourself, *This time is different. This is the exception and it won't end poorly*. For me, it's always ended poorly.

My typical response to these situations is to ignore the guy. I don't look at him, I don't talk to him, and I certainly don't text him. Complete radio silence. I take the time to get him out of my head and out of my heart. I don't want to relapse back into a bad situation, and I want him to hurt the way he hurt me. I want him to realize he screwed up and lost something great. It's a two-fold response: I heal, he hurts. At least, that's my goal.

I lasted through two weeks of silence with Mr. Liar-LiarPantsOnFire until his trying to talk to me at the office finally broke me. I was soon back talking with him. I didn't trust him. I didn't want to have him back in my life. But love is like a drug. Once you have it and experience it, you want more. Even if it makes you sick. You go back because the taste of it was just too good to walk away from. It was as if someone gave me a slice of my favorite cheesecake and let me eat my first bite, then pulled it away before I could finish it. I wasn't done yet. I wanted more.

We talked and laughed like we did before I figured out his lie. He would text me late at night and tell me how beautiful I looked. It made me feel good again, but it was all temporary. Because, you see, when a guy lies to you, especially about something so big, he's shown you his true colors. He's a liar through and through and will always be that way. Let him have the girl he's with and let him be her problem. You deserve better than that, and I deserve better than that.

He eventually moved to be with the girl out of state. I even helped him move his stuff. I'm way too nice. I won't do that again. He told me as he was leaving how much he would miss me and how much he wished he could have both the other girl and me.

Excuse me!? No, thank you. I want a guy who wants to be with me and only me. I left that night knowing I would never see him or talk to him again. The taste wasn't as good as I remembered it to be.

I held true to that promise, too. Like the saying goes, "Fool me once, shame on you; fool me twice, shame on me." I wasn't going to be fooled a third time. The distance helped Mr. LiarLiarPantsOnFire stay out of my life for a good amount of time. He did reach out, though. I'm telling you, they always come back. I ignore those contacts. He made his decision and he could stay with her.

Now, some of you may think he was reaching out to check on me and see how my life was going. Maybe he just wanted to catch up with me because I was important to him in his life. Nah, there's always something more. Even if it is innocent, what's the real purpose? These types of communication only turn into problems. Unless you have to share custody of a dog or child, or there's a real reason to reach out to someone (they have an important legal document of yours, etc.), it's best to shut those relationships off. It's only fair to their significant other and you. You've got to protect yourself.

TheFriendWhoNeverKnewILikedHim

I soon was leaving my job working for the government to join a large corporation in town. I would be meeting even more people, and I couldn't wait. As I was leaving my previous job, I had saved up a lot of time that was paid out to me as I left. I probably should have taken the money and used it as a down-payment for a house, or at the very least put it into an investment account to earn interest and potentially grow. But at that time, I was living that Y.O.L.O. life. I wanted to travel and see the world. I decided to use the money to visit The-FriendWhoNeverKnewILikedHim.

See, TheFriendWhoNeverKnewILikedHim had joined the military and was stationed overseas. I'm talking Asia overseas. I had never been to Asia, and I have a goal of visiting all seven continents before I die. I wanted to check it off my list, which would be the excuse I told everyone both in the U.S. and once I got there. But secretly for me and only a couple friends, there was another reason. I wanted to see if there was any potential connection between me and TheFriend-WhoNeverKnewILikedHim.

It took me awhile to even admit to myself that I had any feelings for TheFriendWhoNeverKnewILiked-Him. I didn't really notice how I felt about him until he called me about a month prior to my trip. He called to wish me a merry Christmas and catch up. He was never really good at responding to my texts in a timely manner, but he was good about calling me up and staying in touch. The phone call this time felt different for me.

He asked about my dating life, per usual. It always comes up in conversations with him, even today. When I told him about my most recent (Mr. LiarLiarPants-OnFire) and reminded him of TheOneYourFriend-Recommends, he apologized for the recommendation and told me he didn't understand why I had such a hard time meeting (and staying) with a guy. He complimented me a lot and told me how smart, caring, and attractive of a woman I was. He basically told me I was a catch and any guy would be lucky to date me.

Now, he's given me similar compliments in the past. Not as direct and strong as this time, though. At least, that's how I felt. I hung up the phone with him, feeling like maybe I had been looking at him all wrong these past years of friendship. Maybe the guy I was supposed to be with had been right in front of my face. I decided I would ramp up our communications. I also spent time putting together a Christmas care package and mailed it out. I then started looking at flights to go visit him. I figured the only way to really know how we felt about each other was meeting in person.

I decided not to disclose to him how I felt until I was there and knew it was the right time. I reached out to him about the flights and asked him what dates would be best for him. Eventually, we worked out a good weekend where he would be free for a couple days and I could stay with him and his friend, who had a bigger apartment. I excitedly booked my fifteen-hour flight out there and took the days off from work. *Asia, here I come!*

It was only two weeks out when I bought my flight to see TheFriendWhoNeverKnewILikedHim. I figured it was now or never, plus flights were cheaper during the winter season. It was soon time to leave, and I was messaging with TheFriendWhoNeverKnewILiked-Him as I waited to board my short flight to Atlanta before the long haul overseas. He kept telling me how he couldn't believe I was coming and he couldn't wait to see me and show me around. I told him I would let him know once I was in Atlanta on my way to see him.

The flight to Atlanta was short, and I spent most of the time wondering about what would happen when I saw him. How he was going to react to me, and whether I could really tell him how I was starting to feel about him. I felt so many emotions, but mostly excitement. No matter what happened between me and The-FriendWhoNeverKnewILikedHim, I was going to be visiting a whole new continent for the first time. The trip was bound to be a good one no matter what.

Then I landed in Atlanta. I gathered all of my stuff and started to make my way through the airport to my international flight. I had a fairly quick turnaround, and Atlanta has a pretty large airport, so I made sure I was almost to my gate before letting The-FriendWhoNeverKnewILikedHim know I had made it safely and would be seeing him in just another flight. Well, sort of.

He wasn't able to meet me at the airport because he told me he still had to work. I was going to land, meet someone for a WIFI hotspot (a portable electronic black box that I could put in my pocket and use for WIFI wherever I was during my time there), buy a bus ticket, find my bus, ride the bus to my stop, and walk to a hostel I had booked for one night. All of this in the dark, with people who spoke a different language. A language written in characters that looked nothing like the English written language. Deep breath. I could do this. I had traveled before; it was possible. Besides, there was nothing he could do since he had to work. So, I would be seeing him in about a day.

We chatted a little when I was almost to my gate about how I would get to my hostel once I landed. Then he hit me with a major blow, one I didn't see coming and I was a bit shocked by. He wrote something along the lines of, *Plus, you'll get to meet this woman whom I'm romantically involved with.* I had to re-read it a couple times to really understand what he was saying.

First, who says, "romantically involved with?" What does that even mean? It's like saying you want to date someone, but you're not really ready to say you want to date them. Second, when did this all happen? I'd legit been talking to him almost every day since he called me a month ago, and this "woman whom he was romantically involved with" never came up once.

I immediately sent a text rampage out to my close friends who knew the real reason I was going on this trip. Did I miss something in the past month? Did I somehow completely ignore hints he may have dropped? Maybe this was the reason he was able to be so open and honest with me about how great he thought I was because if I questioned it, he could just tell me he was already with someone and he meant it as a friend.

Then, in a short thirty minutes, we were being called to board a fifteen-hour flight with no WIFI or phone service, where I knew no one else on the plane. A flight where I would be left alone to think about what exactly just happened and how I was going to handle having to meet TheFriendWhoNeverKnew-ILikedHim, and now apparently his new girlfriend.

If you've never taken a long flight, as you can imagine, it sucks. Maybe if you have the money and can afford a nice reclining plane seat with continual food and drink service, then it's not as bad. But riding in a small metal tube using seats that don't move much past a slight recline with people on either side fighting for a shared arm rest is not fun. Then on top of it, you just found out the guy you're going to see to find out if you could be together is actually already dating someone. This is one of the worst situations you could find yourself in. There was one upside to it all. Unlimited wine in economy.

I had a couple drinks to calm my nerves and try to sleep. It helped a little, but I didn't sleep much at all. Finally, we started to descend to the airport, where I would start my adventure. My trip was going to be a lot different from how I thought it would be when I boarded my first flight. I got off the flight, through customs, found my WIFI guy, boarded my bus, made it off the right stop, and got to my hostel. I was definitely proud of myself. I did it all alone and all in a different language.

As soon as I got to my room, I jumped in the shower and washed off the grossness of sitting on a plane circulating germs for more than half a day. Then I immediately fell into bed and made up for the lack of sleep on the plane ride. I woke up ready to take on the day and meet up with TheFriendWhoNeverKnew-ILikedHim. I told myself this would be a fun trip to see a new country and check another continent off my list. I hadn't completely written off the idea of telling The-FriendWhoNeverKnewILikedHim how I really felt, but I wanted to meet up with him first and meet this "woman he was romantically involved with" to see if I still wanted to tell him.

I met up with him in a coffee shop a couple train stops away and ran to give him a hug. It was a little surreal to be in a different country and seeing him for the first time in almost a year. There was nothing really magical about the hug or meeting him. It was just nice and friendly.

We spent the whole day together. He showed me around the city, including the local military base. The-OneWhomHeWasRomanticallyInvolvedWith was yet to be seen. He told me she had work that day and would meet up with us later that night. He really didn't talk much more about her.

I spent the day meeting his close friends on base and making plans to all meet that night for food and drinks. Then we met up with his friend, who was going to let us stay with him during my time there. I dropped off my bags, and we all headed out for dinner and drinks at the local bars. It was then I met The-OneWhomHeWasRomanticallyInvolvedWith.

She was a native to the country. I gave her a hug when I met her.

I opened my arms wide and said, "Hi! I'm Ashley." As she was hugging me back, she said into my ear, "I know who you are." Not sure if it was a translation issue or this woman was letting me know not to mess with her and TheFriendWhoNeverKnewILikedHim. I shrugged it off and had already pretty much decided I didn't want to tell him how I felt now that she was in the picture. Maybe she knew that I had a secret crush on her man. I actually think a lot of his friends there might've thought it.

His friends kept asking me that night why I decided to come all the way out there and visit for such a short amount of time. I, of course, jumped straight to the reason I had been telling everyone (which was true! It just wasn't the *whole* truth). I told them about my dream to visit all seven continents in the world, and how I had never been to Asia. So, I figured, having a friend there would be the best way to see it, and who knew if I'd get another chance in the future.

That seemed to reassure them, but I could tell one of his friends wasn't completely sold. That friend was a woman. We know. She definitely knew. I wasn't going to admit it, though. Not while TheFriendWho-NeverKnewILikedHim was dating someone else, especially when that girl was at the table with us.

The rest of the trip was fun and interesting, but also at times exhausting and annoying. TheFriendWho-NeverKnewILikedHim brought the TheOneWhom-HeWasRomanticallyInvolvedWith pretty much everywhere we went. When she wasn't with us, he continued to ask me my opinion of her and whether I liked her. I was honest with him about that, at least. I told him she was a nice girl, but not someone I would choose to be a close friend of mine.

See, I try and surround myself with strong, ambitious, passionate women who are confident and independent.

TheOneWhomHeWasRomanticallyInvolvedWith did not fit that criteria. She cowered into TheFriendWho-NeverKnewILikedHim's shoulder at the sight of a cartoon video character dying on the TV. She told me she didn't know how to navigate the subway system in her own country because it was just too confusing. Plus, she did the whole getting in the way of me trying to see if there was anything between me and TheFriendWho-NeverKnewILikedHim.

Don't get me wrong. She really was a nice girl. She took me and TheFriendWhoNeverKnewILikedHim out to a traditional tea ceremony and we made cultural dolls. I just wouldn't want to be her best friend. I told him, too, what I thought shouldn't matter. I wasn't the one who was spending the rest of my life with her. It was his life and his choice. It wasn't the answer he was looking for, but it was the best I could give him.

I left Asia with a goodbye hug to TheFriendWho-NeverKnewILikedHim, and to this day his name remains. I never told him how I felt about him. I would find out later that he actually was off work when I landed in Asia and would have been able to pick me up from the airport and make sure I made it to my hostel safely. Instead, he had met up with TheOneWhomHeWasRomanticallyInvolvedWith.

That was the final straw for me. I had let go of any possibility of us being together. He had lied to me and put me second to someone else. He did this to me when I was visiting him, in a foreign country, not knowing the language or where I was going.

Ultimately, things tend to work out in the end. I don't think if I had told him how I felt it would have changed anything. He went on to marry TheOneWhomHe-WasRomanticallyInvolvedWith.

Then they divorced. Now he's with someone new. Through it all, we've remained friends, and he continues to question me about why I can't seem to find someone to date. Little does he know he is part of that story, and he will probably forever remain TheFriendWhoNeverKnewI-LikedHim. Unless he actually reads this book (doubtful) and figures it out (probably not happening).

TheOneYouMeetWhenYou'reNotLooking

One of the things people like to tell me—usually people who are already in long-term relationships—is that I will find the person I'm supposed to be with when I stop looking for him. As if I am going along in life constantly wondering who I should date next and if the guy across from me on the bus might be my future lover. They're also somewhat saying, "Don't worry about it, just live your life and the right person will come around." Those same people also tend to be the ones that constantly ask if you've met anyone or are dating someone new. As if you shouldn't worry about it, but you should when you see them because they're worrying about it for you.

Then I met TheOneYouMeetWhenYou'reNot-Looking. It was on a typical weekend night out in Columbus, Ohio. I had joined a dance group for a lacrosse team in town. Part of the requirement of volunteering for the team and dancing all day was to go downtown for the after party. We were even required to dress up in nice black dresses. I'm still not sure why we had such a dress code.

On this particular night, I didn't feel like drinking or finding a ride back home afterwards. So I decided I'd drive with my roommate to the bar and just drink water. I also didn't think we'd be staying out too late. We were usually excused before midnight. I think the program meant for it to be fun, but really it just ended up feeling like a requirement. About an hour after we got to the bar, I received a text from one of my friends in town. She was out with her fiancé at a bar just a short walk away and wanted to see if I could meet up with them.

I hadn't seen her much since she moved to town and decided to try and convince the other girls I was with to go with me. They all agreed that a change of scenery would be nice and followed me a few blocks to the nearby bar. It was Pride weekend, and the bars were packed with people. I found her at the front of the bar, already well ahead of me with alcohol. She was excited to see me but admitted there was another reason she had texted me to meet up. There was a guy close by who she wanted to introduce. She had just met him that night herself, but really liked him and thought we would hit it off.

I laughed and rolled my eyes a little. Many of my friends had tried to set me up in the past, and there was usually no chemistry at all between me and the guy they knew. I also couldn't tell if this was her genuine thought process, or fueled by the alcohol she had been drinking that night. Before I knew it, she had dragged this poor guy over to me and said, "This is my friend, Ashley. Ashley, this is TheOneYouMeetWhenYou're-NotLooking." I shook his hand, smiled, and said, "Hi."

I asked him how he spelled his name, and he confirmed for me that he had the same name as Mr. Italiano. Not that generalizing is a good thing, but I can say most of the guys who have the name these two share and spell it the same way are no good. They're fine to befriend and joke with, but don't pursue a relationship with them. It doesn't work out.

We talked for a little, and then I walked away to rejoin my other friends who came with me to the bar. I debated going back to talk with him, but there was just something about him that made me want to talk with him more. I quickly went back to find out if there was more to him than the name his parents had given him. I found out he was celebrating pride weekend with his cousin and wore bright colored beads around his neck. That alone was a huge bonus for me. He was comfortable in his own skin and didn't judge other people for their decisions about love.

He was also really outgoing, fun, and friendly. He said hi to people as they walked past us. There was one turn off, though. He had a cigarette stuck behind his ear. It's a deal-breaker for me. I pointed it out to him and asked why he had it. He assured me he only smoked when he drank and didn't make a habit out of it. I believed him, but knew time would tell the truth.

Soon my friends were looking to leave, and I was their ride, so I gave him a hug goodbye and told him I enjoyed meeting him. He agreed and asked for my number. I gave it to him and quickly left with a huge smile on my face.

Maybe everyone was right. That night, I really did go out with friends and I wasn't thinking about anything or anyone. I just wanted to have a good night out. Then all of this happened. Was there really something to meeting someone when you're not looking?

He texted me that night to tell me how he really liked meeting me, and I responded in agreement. I smiled the whole ride home and went to bed happy and excited by what had happened that night. A giddiness for things that had yet to come. We hadn't made any plans, though, so only time would tell if he felt the same about me.

I waited to hear from him that weekend, and sure enough, he texted to ask me out on a date. He wanted to take me out for dinner to a local sushi restaurant. This alone was a big gesture. You'd think dinner wasn't much, but dating nowadays tends to be mostly getting a drink or coffee, and ultimately the bill is usually split and no food is shared. Not only did he suggest dinner, he also offered to pick me up and take me to the restaurant.

As kind as it was for him to offer me a ride, I declined and told him I would meet him there. I am a huge true crime fan and I worked in a prosecutor's office. I like to really get to know a person before they pick me up in their car. If my friend was close with him and I trusted my friend's opinion, then I'd accept the ride. My friend in this case had only met him that night at the bar. I decided to just drive separately and see what happened.

He dressed up and looked really nice. We both selected a variety of sushi and split it with each other. He was adventurous and made me laugh several times. He had also traveled outside the country, which was unusual for most of the guys I had met in Ohio. On top of it all, he paid for our dinner that night. Another unusual event in the dating world.

Neither of us wanted the night to end, and he suggested a nearby bar for a nightcap. I agreed, and we caravanned over to the other location. He told me a lot about himself that night, including a nickname he had for underwear. I felt comfortable with him and I really thought he might be the one I would finally talk about as my boyfriend. At the end of the date, my guard was still up, though, because so many guys ran from me.

As we were closing the bar tab, he looked at me and said, "Not to be weird, but this reminds me of how my parents met." I'm going to be honest; I was a bit shocked by this statement. I'm also really bad at hiding my feelings on my face, so I'm sure he could tell I was bit caught off guard. He laughed a little and said never mind. I couldn't tell if it was a line he used to try and get a girl to go home with him or if he said it because he truly was falling for me. I figured only time would tell.

He walked me to my car and I gave him a hug. I didn't even kiss him that night, but I assured him I had a great time and wanted to see him again. He said he felt the same way. Soon, we were going on our second date together, and I found out he lived not so far from me. Literally only a couple blocks away. Coincidence, or fate?

We dated for a few months, and soon I was leaving for a trip to Norway. He had been a little distant with me beforehand and I wasn't sure where things were going with him. I was reaching a point where I wanted to know if we were dating exclusively or move on from whatever it was we were doing. I figured I would go on my trip and ask him once I returned home. I was heading overseas for a friend's wedding, and two of my friends were joining me. We had been planning the trip for months, and I couldn't wait.

The trip was amazing, and while at the wedding reception, I met a really cute Norwegian guy. We talked for a little outside the reception hall, and then he looked for me inside for a dance. All I could think about was TheOneYouMeetWhenYou'reNot-Looking, and I didn't want to hurt whatever it was I had with him. I stayed clear of that handsome Norwegian man that night. It's something I still regret to this day.

See, when I returned home bringing TheOneYou-MeetWhenYou'reNotLooking chocolates from my trip, I found out he was no longer looking for a relationship. He had been asked by his office to take a job in, believe it or not, Asia, and he would be leaving within a few months. Since he was leaving and moving there for a year, he didn't want to have a relationship with me. He had been avoiding seeing me for this reason. Once again, a man I fell for didn't want to be with me. I thought I had met someone different for once. I thought maybe things were different this time. Unfortunately, just like almost all of the other ones, this relationship came to an end, and I didn't have a choice in the matter.

The Wedding Date

It was about this time, back in Ohio, when I decided I was over dating and being single. I decided to start a podcast and blog about modern dating, titled "How Are You Still Single?" I wanted more people to understand how hard dating is now, and maybe if they listened, they would stop asking so many of us how we could still be single. Of course, I didn't think it would be interesting to give only my thoughts, and I wanted to make sure I got honest opinions. So I decided to go out to bars and conduct live interviews with people by recording them on my cell phone. This way I could get pretty honest answers (based on how late it was in the night) and people could remain anonymous.

I think I've started to change some people's minds, and I've definitely brought a group of people together to know they're not struggling in the single world alone. The other thing that happened was I met a lot of new people, including new guys. One of those guys I met and interviewed was TheWeddingDate.

He proudly answered my questions and let me record him. Then, when I was done, he asked me how he could contact me and I gave him my podcast's email address. He said, "No, I mean your phone number." I laughed and gave it to him, thinking it wasn't a big deal. I didn't talk to him much more that night because I was more concerned with getting additional interviews for my show. I couldn't waste any time.

I ended up seeing him a little later that night at another bar, but we didn't talk. I figured he took my number but wasn't going to use it. As if it was a bet he had with his friends that he could get it. It didn't really matter to me, though. I didn't know him and probably would never run into him again, so I brushed it off.

Then the next day, I got a text from him asking me out on a date. I was surprised to hear from him and that he would want to take me on a date. I agreed, and we met up at a local bar for a drink, but I also made plans to meet my friends later that night. It's always good to have an exit plan for dates. You just never know how they will go, and you do not want to get stuck for hours on a terrible one.

The date actually ended up going really well, and I ended up skipping one of the meetups I had scheduled to stay a bit longer with him. He was really caring and seemed interested in me and what I was doing. Plus, he knew about half the people at the bar.

Apparently he went to high school with one of the owners. I ended up getting introduced to several people from his past that night on our very first date together. As strange and awkward as that sounds, he made it seem very normal.

I thanked him for my drink and left after a few hours. He texted me shortly after I left to tell me he really enjoyed our date and wanted to take me out again. For our second date, he took me to the state fair to eat a crap-ton of bad fried food. Before the date, I told him I had to run to my friend's birthday party for a little bit and then I would meet him back at my place. He said he would just go with me to the birthday party and then we could head to the fair.

I was shocked. Most guys I've dated don't want to be introduced to my friends on the second date, or even the fifth date. I was happy he wanted to go and thought this could be the guy that's different from all the rest.

I introduced him to several of my friends at the party and he fit right in. I couldn't believe he wanted to meet my friends and wasn't weird about it. Most of the guys I had dated would've been freaked out and run away if I suggested going to a party with my other friends. TheWeddingDate seemed to be different and more confident in himself and not so scared off by normal things. I was excited to get to know him better. We spent the rest of the night walking around the fair, holding hands and eating a ton of food.

Afterwards, we didn't want the night to end and he took me out to his favorite bar. He then had his cousin come out to meet us. I was a little nervous meeting his family so soon, but I thought maybe this was a sign that he was taking our dates seriously and he wasn't a guy who would tell me later he didn't want a relationship. His cousin was also really nice and we had a fun night with her. We ended up giving her a ride home and then he walked me up to my apartment.

We stayed up late talking on my couch that night, and he left in the late hours of the morning. It was really comfortable and exciting. I thought this was how it's supposed to go, where you don't want to leave each other and you could spend all night talking. We continued to see each other, having fun together on some very non-traditional dates.

We spent a date together riding electric scooters around downtown. He showed me places he used to go to as a kid in high school, and it felt like we were kids again. We also went ice skating together. He used to play hockey in high school and was really good at skating. He even went with me to a retail store late one night to help me buy decorations for a coworker's birthday just so he could spend a little more time with me.

He would listen to my podcast each week and give me feedback about how much he liked it. He was my cheerleader and a huge supporter of my decision to produce a podcast. I felt so lucky to meet him. I then decided to ask him to go to a coworker's wedding with me.

I was a little nervous about asking him because I felt like it was a big step. Luckily, he said he would be honored and had the perfect suit to wear. He actually had me send a picture of my dress to him so he could match his tie and socks to the color of it. Who was this guy?

On the weekend of my coworker's wedding, I had a different wedding in Chicago the Friday and Saturday before. He spent the whole weekend texting with me and telling me how pretty I looked in my wedding outfits. The other bridesmaids could see how happy he made me and were hoping it worked out between the two of us. They would tell me how it reminded them of how they were when they met their husbands.

Soon, I was driving back to Ohio to meet up with him and bring him to the wedding as my date. It was the first wedding I had ever taken a date, especially one that I could actually see as my boyfriend. Finally.

He met me at my apartment in time to go to the wedding venue. One of my other coworkers and his husband picked us up to take us to the wedding so we could both drink and not worry about driving home that night. He met all of my coworkers and won most of them over. He made sure I always had a drink, put his arm around me during the ceremony, and wiped my sunglasses so they were clear for me to see. All of this without me asking him. Even another one of my co-workers and his wife said how cute we looked and remembered how they used to put their arms around each other, too.

We smiled at the dinner table together, and he easily talked to everyone at the table. Then they played the couple's game where the couple is seated back-to-back and held up a shoe to show who they thought would fit the descriptions better. Things like, "who is the better driver" or, "who is the better cook." He would tap me on the leg when they asked questions and answered them for us. Those little touches and comments made me think he thought we were also moving in that direction. We even danced the night away on the dance floor together. He was a great dancer and made me smile the whole night.

All of my coworkers were excited for me and told me they thought he was a great guy. I felt the same way and thought this could really be something special. All of my coworkers felt that way except one. He didn't tell me at that time, but eventually he did. See, the wedding was the last date I went on with The-WeddingDate. We would see each other once more when I asked to give him his birthday gift before I left on a work flight to Texas. I gave him a pair of *Jurassic Park* socks because it was his favorite movie and he was going to see the sequel for his birthday.

He thanked me for the gift and we texted here and there afterwards, but eventually I asked him to meet up with me and he declined. He didn't call me or see me in person, nope. He texted me to tell me I was a great girl, but he didn't see a future with me. It's always the compliment along with those crushing words. Sure, I'm great, but apparently not great enough for him to want to actually be in a relationship with me. Not even great enough for him to call or meet me in person to tell me he was ending it.

The coworker who didn't like him told me he was too into himself and I deserved someone better. I look back now and believe him. At the time, it was really hard. I didn't understand what had happened, and like all the other guys, he left me with unanswered questions. All I knew was that he wasn't the one.

TheMuchOlderMan

After TheWeddingDate, I took a break from dating again. It's important to take beaks! It's hard to really trust another person after you let your guard down with someone and they text you that they don't want to date you anymore without much of any explanation. I took this time to go out with my friends and have fun nights out. I didn't go out looking for anyone or wanting to meet anyone. I went to standup shows, workout classes, happy hours, and different bars. I was living my life and not worrying about anything.

One warm summer night, I went out with a friend to a bar and ordered a drink that said it was for two-to-four people. In reality, I think it was really for six-to-eight people. It came out in a large wine bucket with at least ten neon colored crazy straws to drink from it. My friend and I both had our eyes wide open when we saw it. We made it about halfway through the drink before we started offering it to people sitting next   to   us.   One   of   those   people   was TheMuchOlderMan.

He never looked his age. He always seemed much more my age than his when we met and when we hung out. I actually thought he liked my friend, and he took both my number and my friend's number that night. It was a bit confusing, but I didn't think much of it and wanted my friend to meet someone new. I was still on the getting-over-TheWeddingDate-wanting-to-be-single train.

I didn't think we'd hear from TheMuchOlderMan again, but soon he was texting with us to meet up. It was a group text with my friend. Maybe he really was just looking to meet new people in the city. We invited him out and he joined my friend, and a couple of our other friends, and me for some queso, nachos, and margaritas shortly after. He was really nice and even paid for all of our drinks. There was something about him that really intrigued me. I definitely wanted to see him again.

The next time we met, I invited him over to co-host with me on my podcast. He met me at my place in the morning and joined me for breakfast. After recording the show, he asked if I wanted to get a drink, and I didn't have any plans so I agreed. We stopped off at his condo downtown first to let his dog out and then headed out for drinks at a nearby bar. We met up with some of my friends there and then moved on to have pizza and wine at another restaurant. Then we played darts at another bar and rode an electric scooter together back to his home to let his dog out again. While we were playing darts, we overheard that a band was playing in town, and after letting his dog out for the second time, we decided to scalp tickets and go.

It was at the concert we shared a kiss. I was the one that made the move. It was so easy talking with him and hanging out with him. We had spent the whole day together, and it felt like it had only been a couple hours. He returned my kiss, and we held each other for the entire concert. We then went back to his place to take his dog out again. I ended up passing out on his couch while we watched a TV series together. He pulled a blanket over me and went to sleep in his bedroom. In the morning, he walked me back to my apartment and was a complete gentleman.

It was a whirlwind of a day, and I wasn't sure what would happen between us in the future. See, we were fourteen years apart. It was quite a large age gap, but it really didn't feel that way when I was with him. Besides, you always hear of couples who are together with even larger age gaps. I really didn't think it mattered, as long as we cared about each other. We would text each other all the time after that day, and he always knew what to say to make me laugh.

We hung out a couple more times, making chili together for dinner and going out one night to meet his friends. We could talk about anything and text for hours. Then he got distant with me. He didn't text me as much, and I didn't know what had happened. I asked to meet up with him, and he agreed.

It was then he told me in a roundabout way that he didn't want to full-on date me. He wanted to keep dating other people because he wanted to find someone to marry, basically indicating he didn't think I was the one without saying it to me. He also kissed me that night as we were leaving the bar. It was very confusing.

We still talked after that night, but it was different. I thought with his vague statements, he may eventually want to date me seriously, and we were still getting to know each other. He kept bringing up our large age gap, though. There was nothing I could say or do to change our ages. Eventually, I started applying for jobs in Chicago. I needed to get out of Columbus. I couldn't deal with one more guy telling me how great I was but not wanting to date me. I needed a fresh start and a new city with more options in it.

Then I got an interview for a job in Chicago. He wished me luck with the interview and even called me afterwards to ask me how it went and help get me through the long drive back to Ohio. I ended up getting that job, and he was sad to see me leave, but now he had an additional excuse for us not to date— the fact I was now going to be living two states away. He still wasn't clear about it, though.

He kept saying how he wanted to move out of Ohio, and maybe he would follow me to Chicago because he had worked there before and loved it. We also met before I left and had lunch together, and he got me a card saying we had "unfinished business" and he couldn't wait to visit me in Chicago, along with a stuffed bunny to remind me of him. All things to make me think maybe he was considering continuing the relationship.

I thought maybe there was a chance for him to move closer to me, but it didn't happen. Instead he started dating someone else. He, just like the others, texted me. He texted to tell me he had started seeing someone seriously and said it was hard and awkward to tell me. He still wanted to be my friend, though. Most of them always want to be my friend. It's too hard to be friends, though. It also doesn't make much sense to me when you've had feelings for each other.

He actually called me two nights in a row to convince me we should still be friends and told me I would change my mind about it. I didn't change my mind, and I haven't talked to him since. More because when we talked and said our goodbyes, he told me I had made things with him into more than they were. I completely disagreed, and I felt led-on and hurt. If he really wanted to be friends, then he should have been clear about it months prior. Once again, I was single and confused, but at least this time I was in a new city with way more opportunities.

TheOne

I was back in Chicago and finally getting into the groove of things, with new plans almost every night. I signed up for any and every company, volunteer, or team event to get to know more people. I was back on the dating apps, trying to meet as many different people as possible. It was amazing. I soaked up every minute I could.

My office was the traditional open-desk concept, where everyone can mingle and interact with each other. I have a love/hate relationship with the layout. There are moments when I welcome and enjoy the distractions, and other times when I could really use the quiet time to concentrate on work. The one good thing is that it makes it easier to meet new people, and I took full advantage of it.

I was working in the financial industry, which automatically means most of the people in my office were men. Normally, in Ohio, a majority of them would already be engaged or married at this point in their lives. In Chicago, a good number were still single or not quite to the engagement point in their life. Eventually, the sun finally came out for Summer, and people stayed around for a drink after work in the office or went out to the many bars nearby. I was finally starting to really get to know people.

There were a couple guys at the office I was interested in getting to know a little better. I usually hung around a little longer at the office so I could grab a drink with them afterwards. It never really turned into anything, though, and I continued to go out on dates with guys I met on the dating apps. I also joined a couple sand volleyball teams to meet more people, too. The app dates were just blah, though. There wasn't anyone that really got my attention yet.

Then one day after work, I was out with a bunch of guys and trying to hit on one of them. He didn't seem to notice, or maybe he just wasn't interested in me. It was then another guy, TheOne, suggested that I exchange numbers with the guy I had been trying to flirt with. I had made a bet with the guy I was interested in that I could make it back to my apartment in forty minutes and sending a photo from my apartment in my outfit was the way I could prove it. I tried to feign ignorance and started to say how we didn't need to exchange numbers and we were just making a bet. But secretly, I did want it to happen.

I was surprised TheOne could see that I was interested in the other guy when it seemed like the other guy couldn't tell at all. TheOne kept telling me, "You're welcome." I laughed and told him I didn't know what he was talking about, but I knew that he knew. Who was this guy? I had been trying to give this other guy signs I was interested in him for weeks, and TheOne figured it out in one night. He actually paid attention to what other people were doing. I honestly would've rather dated him than this guy, who couldn't or didn't want to make any move on me.

Sadly, he was dating someone else and off limits. Isn't that always how it goes? I left that night and won the bet (according to me). If you ask the other guy, I lost. Either way, I met TheOne, and that night would later mean more to me than it did at the time.

I would say hi to TheOne at work and talk a little here and there with him after work, but nothing more than that—until I signed up to volunteer at an event that had us making food together. I showed up a little late because of work I had to get done at the office. I rushed in and was told to go to the dessert area. I grabbed a drink and started to head out of the room and was immediately lost. I started walking down a hallway, and suddenly TheOne was right behind me.

He asked me what I was doing. I told him I didn't know where we were supposed to go for the desserts. He was heading to the restroom, but if I waited for him, he would show me when he got out. I agreed, and he took me to our room.

I learned a lot about TheOne that night. He was really outgoing and loved talking to everyone. He introduced himself to all the volunteers there that night and asked them about themselves. We talked for a bit together, too. I told him about the wedding I was attending in Norway in just a couple months. He was jealous and actually wanted to come with me. I knew he was joking, but it was the exact reaction I was looking for from a guy. I wanted a guy to be excited to travel overseas to go to a wedding with me.

He told me about his own travels—how he took six months and traveled all over Europe and parts of Africa. We had both been to several of the same countries, including Greece, Scotland, and Italy. We talked about our favorite things from those places. He was adventurous, sincere, kind, and funny. I left that night wanting to get to know him even more. I felt a connection with him but chalked it up to him being so outgoing and able to connect with everyone in the room. Besides, I was pretty sure he was still with his elusive girlfriend who I had yet to see. I shrugged. I figured if it was meant to happen, it would.

Then, one week, I noticed he was acting a little different than usual. He was staying after work later, and I saw him one night taking the elevator to the roof. I asked him what he was doing and he said he was just going up for a break. It seemed odd to me. I wondered then if something had happened between him and his girlfriend. I could see the pain in his eyes, but I wasn't sure what it was about. I said goodbye and headed out with my coworkers for a drink. One of them even noticed the connection between us and said something about it on our way out. I laughed and told her how he was taken and it was nothing.

Then, one night, TheOne and I were leaving the office at the same time. I still noticed that there was something off about him. He just wasn't the same as the other nights I had hung out with him. I was going over to a bar next door to meet up with a bunch of my friends and say goodbye to one of their friends who was in town visiting.

He told me he was headed to the gym to work off some steam. I asked him if he was okay, and he assured me he would be okay. I told him I was there for him if he ever needed someone to talk with about anything. He thanked me, and we parted to go our separate ways.

Then, just as I was a couple steps away, I thought I'd turn around and invite him out for a drink. I was already going to be early and I could use the company while I waited for my friends to arrive. I also figured he could probably use a drink. I quickly turned back, hustled around the corner, and called his name. I wasn't sure I'd stop him in time. He heard me, though, and turned around. I asked him to join me for a drink, my treat. I could tell he had a hard day, maybe week, and figured I'd try to help make it a little better.

He fought it a little; he really wanted to be alone. Then he finally shrugged and said, "Why not?" I agreed with him, and he followed me to the rooftop bar nearby. We took a seat at the bar, and I texted my friends to let them know I was there and would try to save some seats. We both got an old fashioned and talked with each other like we'd been friends forever.

I learned a lot about him that night and I opened up to him about a lot of things. He spoke Spanish with my friends and had been to one of their home countries for volunteer work one summer. I was really impressed by him and wished I could be with someone like him. Before all of my friends got there, though, he told me what had been causing him to have such a hard time lately. His girlfriend had broken up with him.

She had told him the same thing all the guys from my past had told me. How he was such a great person and she cared about him a lot, but she didn't want to date him. I smirked and told him I knew exactly how that felt. He then made some comments about how all girls just want to date dark-haired guys—I'm sure a dig at me for the guy I had tried to flirt with earlier and he had helped me get his number.

I rolled my eyes and assured him I didn't date guys based on their looks, and that I had liked him and would date him if he was available. For once, I was actually straightforward and told a guy that I liked him and would date him. It felt good. I'm sure the alcohol helped me with a little of my courage, and he seemed a bit surprised by my confidence, too. He didn't really react to my statement at the moment, but he smiled really big.

I also commiserated with him on the terrible feeling of hearing someone tell you how amazing you are but not wanting to actually be with you. How it's really confusing, and arguably much harder to move on from than when someone just tells you they don't think you're compatible. The connection I had felt before with him was becoming even more apparent to both of us that night. It was like we had known each other all of our lives, but we were just then finally meeting.

I still had my guard up with him. I really liked him and wanted to see what would happen, but I was also well aware of the possible problems. We worked together, not in the same company, but for affiliated companies. Which is basically like working for the same company, but a little better than having offices just a few doors away from each other like with Mr. LiarLiarPants-OnFire. Plus, he was clearly still getting over his ex. It's always dangerous dating someone when they haven't fully healed from a previous relationship. There's always a concern they're not being themselves, and of course the ex could potentially change their mind and ask for them back.

I didn't think about all of those things that night, though. I was enjoying our conversation and watching him fit in so well with my friends, who finally made it to the bar. We drank way too much that night, but it got us to open up and share a lot about ourselves with each other. I think that brought us close quickly.

I didn't know what to expect after that night. Whether what I felt was also how he felt or if he was just drowning in his sorrows that night. We texted each other almost the whole next day, and he asked to hang out again after work. For some reason, I wanted to see him. Usually, I need my space and time to get to know a guy. I don't want to see him more than once a week, really. This was different. I had a taste of something real, and I wanted more of it. I agreed to ride the train back with him to his neighborhood and grab a drink.

We sat down in the back of a typical small neighborhood bar where he knew the bartenders. He bought me my drinks and we talked more about our lives and our dreams. He could tell I was holding back a little and unsure about what was happening. I told him I didn't trust what was happening right now, and I thought he should be out dating a bunch of different people to figure out what he wanted now that he was newly single. He disagreed. He said he had already done that and wasn't interested in getting back out in the dating world.

He understood my concerns and didn't know what he would do if his ex asked to get back together. I appreciated his honesty and figured I would take it all one day at a time. The night flew by, and soon we were spending Saturday together, too. He came over to my apartment with Chipotle and we watched TV all day while cuddling on the couch. It was so nice to have him there. I was falling for him more each time we saw each other.

I wasn't annoyed by him like I had been with guys in the past. I didn't mind seeing him at work and I wanted to see him again afterwards. We worked out together and did work together at Starbucks. We went to the local Polish and German festivals. I was finally doing the things I wanted to do in the city with someone I wanted to date. I started to finally realize what everyone else had always told me I should look for in a relationship.

It was easy with him. I was comfortable with him and I could be myself with him. He supported me and challenged me when I talked with him about issues at work or with friends. He made me a better person. We listened to each other and worked together whenever we dealt with a problem, whether it was driving through traffic or dealing with rude people at the Chicago Planetarium. We balanced each other out.

I had to get a mole removed shortly after we met, and he was there for me to make sure I took care of my stitches properly. He was gentler with my wound than I think I could have been. Even though it was a small cut, he knew how much it freaked me out and made sure I was okay and it healed properly. He was my rock, my partner, and my best friend.

We had both talked to our families about each other, and he told me his mom was really excited to meet me. We even talked about spending time together over the holidays and meeting the family. Soon we were talking about moving in together. We were already spending almost every day together and it felt right.

I know some people thought we were moving a little fast, but as the saying goes, "When you know, you know." I was starting to really understand what all of my friends who were engaged or married were trying to tell me. Once it's right, you realize how the other people you dated were not right for you and you wonder why you spent so much time with them. If only I could've seen the future then.

I wanted to see him every day and come home to him every night. I wanted him to meet all of my friends and leave parties early with me to go home and just be by ourselves. We had fun together no matter what we did. Whether it was going on a date by ourselves or going out for drinks with friends after playing a game of volleyball. It was everything I had always imagined. Finally.

Sometimes, it really is just about timing: you and someone else are in the right place at the right time to meet and fall in love. He was the second boyfriend in my life I'd said "I love you" to, and I saw him being the last one—you know, barring unforeseen circumstances. I didn't know what our wedding would look like quite yet. I knew it was going to be a ton of fun. We both loved to dance and sing out loud. We would sing along to songs as we drove to run errands on the weekends. No judgment on the wrong words or off-key sounds (by me). I couldn't imagine my life without him.

***

It was finally time to start looking for condos to buy together. We wanted space for family and friends to visit and for us each to work on our side hustles. We were both ambitious and dreamers who did the hard work after long hours in the office or on the weekend. He paid close attention to the rings I wore, and any time I changed one up, he'd ask about it. I finally made it to the place I'd always wanted to be in with someone. It all felt right and made sense. I was at peace and happy. I had found my lifelong partner.

I finally didn't have to answer all the questions about how I could still be single because I was no longer single. I met someone who saw me for who I was and actually wanted to be with me. It's hard to explain even now. Soon we would be making plans to celebrate our love with all of our friends and family, my sister by my side giving a toast at the reception and dancing all night with TheOne. We would shut down the place, and the workers would usher us out to our ride with the obnoxious white paint on the back window reading…

JUST…

Kidding!

***

I hope you have a look of confusion on your face right now. Perhaps you've flipped the pages back and re-read the past few paragraphs. You were looking for the words "JUST MARRIED." You were sure you just read a love story meant to be shared for a lifetime. One that brought a smile to your face and calmed your uneasiness that I would end the book still single. A sort of reassurance that it will work out in the end.

I wish I could give that to you. What you're feeling in this minute is how I felt in this relationship. I truly believed it would turn into marriage and a lifelong partnership. Someone to share my dreams and travels with for the rest of my life.

It hurts, doesn't it? You may even be a little mad at me, as if I led you on and welcomed you into this safe space with the protagonist. You wanted me to succeed like all those childhood and holiday movies you watch. I did, too. I was crushed.

I cried, a lot. I ate several chocolate covered donuts. I felt betrayed, just as you do now. This is how so many single people feel. When you ask us at the dinner table or family gatherings why we're not with someone, why we're still single, this is the story we replay in our mind. We want you to walk through it with us.

Perhaps then, you'll stop asking and realize we don't have an answer for you.

See, "The One" was really the TheOneWhoWent-BackToHisEx. We shared a whirlwind relationship that was like nothing I had ever experienced. I shared stories of him with my family and friends, telling them I thought I finally understood what I should've been looking for all of these years.

He did everything right. We spent almost every day together after the night at the rooftop bar. Everything I wrote about him was true. All of it until the asterisks. Before we got to the next step in our relationship, he received a text. A text from his ex-girlfriend who had told him she didn't want to date him anymore. She had changed her mind. She wanted him back.

Now, I have some saving grace knowing it wasn't an easy decision for him. He took a few weeks to decide whether he wanted to stay with me or give his ex-girlfriend another shot. I suppose that time he took made me feel like what we had was real and he did feel the same as I did. But in the end, I wasn't her. I didn't have the years and memories she had with him. He decided to take her back.

He told me I was enough, what we had was real, that he cared about me a lot, and if we had more time together he may have made a different decision. But no matter what he said, his actions made his words feel meaningless. I felt like I wasn't good enough. I thought I had finally figured out what love was all about and what a real relationship should feel like, and all of a sudden it was over. I was alone again, right before the holidays.

Yup. I let my guard down once again. I knew I was taking risks, but I thought maybe this time it would pay off. I was wrong, again. I wasn't the girl the guy picked to be with the rest of his life. My heart had once again been handed over to another person who took it and made one more crack, only deeper this time.

He said the same thing to me at the end that brought us together at the beginning. He told me how incredible I am, how amazing I am, how he cares about me so much, but he couldn't be with me. Of course, he still wanted to be friends. He didn't want to lose me in his life. The pain was too much for me, though. This was a completely different situation than any guy in my past. The feelings were still there for both of us, I was pretty sure. He just had two girls after him this time and chose her over me.

All of my friends took my side, of course, and told me he wasn't worth it and I just need to let go and move on. It's easy for a lot of them to say this to me when they haven't experienced the same. It's much harder to walk away from someone who doesn't have any other reason for leaving you except there's someone else that came back. It's even harder knowing how amazing it is to have something so special and having to let it all go.

You start to question if it's ever actually going to work out in the end. You start to question if it's really worth the pain at the end. This is the most important time to focus on yourself and give yourself time to heal. Even if there isn't someone else in the future, you still have an amazing life in front of you with great friends and family. It's hard to see it at this moment, but in time you will heal, just as I am healing now.

6|Keep Loving Yourself

(...And Stop Asking Us How We Could Still Be Single!)

There you have it. There's most of my dating life. What I hope you read throughout my love stories, were the amazing trips I took and beautiful memories I made with so many people. Those are the most important moments of my life. I also gained a lot of life lessons and didn't let the fact I was single get in the way of pursuing my adventurous goals in life. I hope you do the same.

See, these were my love stories with a different ending. They are some of many love stories shared in the world. Most of the ones you hear about, though, are those in the movies or told by the best man or maid of honor at a wedding reception. Those are the ones that are told with the happy endings. They are stories of two people committing to each other for the rest of their lives.

The stories in this book feel the same deep connection as those love stories. They're just never usually told in public. They're kept inside diaries, told in therapy sessions, or hidden in the past, never to be shared with anyone. These are my love stories. Love stories without the typical happy ending. They're not just my stories, though. They're the stories of all those women and men in the world that continue to be asked, "How are you still single?"

Now you have a little idea of why we're still single. It's not the same reason for everyone. We all have our different stories. One day, we hope we finally have the story without an ending. A story we can share with our family and friends. A story that will continue to develop for a lifetime. Until then, we do our best to learn from our past and make better choices in the future.

The hardest part about the end of these love stories (the breakups) is what your ex says to you when they do it. When they don't give you a reason. No. It's them telling you how amazing you are. How you're incredible and they're really going to miss you. It's confusing. I think it hurts more than a simple, "I don't see us working out," or "We're just not the right fit."

Why? Because it leaves you wondering what happened. Why someone who thinks so highly of you doesn't want to be with you. Your friends and family also keep telling you how much of a catch you are and how lucky someone would be to have you in their life. You start to question if they're all lying to you. If the guy really feels that way about you, then why is he leaving?

Then from others, there's always the "I hope we can still be friends" line. I've fallen for it more times than I'd like to admit. But for the one who was broken up with, there are still feelings. Those feelings will be around for some time depending on the connection you had with the person. Plus, when they tell you how amazing you are and they still want to see you, the first thing you think is that they'll change their mind. You should stick around and be friends; then they'll see what they're missing and want you back. Wrong.

Instead, you'll hang on to your feelings for them longer, and things still won't change. It's important at this moment to let go and cut off all communication. I mean, don't even look at photos of them or their social media profiles. It's not going to be easy. It's hard to suddenly lose someone who was such a big part of your life. Someone you might have pictured spending the rest of your life with.

These are the times when you really notice people asking how you could still be single. As you're also questioning what happened, especially when your ex told you how much you meant to them. While you're trying your best to smile and pretend like you're okay, but deep down, you're hurt, sad, and once again alone.

We have an internal struggle questioning ourselves about every detail of the relationship and where it went wrong. We question the conversations we had with our significant other and at times blame ourselves for the relationship ending. We don't need you to ask us even more questions, because we already ask ourselves enough.

We promise you, if we are with someone we know will finally be coming home with us to meet our family and friends, we'll let you know. In the meantime, know we're struggling. Know we're not sure why it's taking us longer to find someone to date or marry. Be there for us to lean on and lend an ear to listen to us. That's what we need.

For all of you struggling in the dating world, don't give up. Don't let not being with someone take away from what you want to do with your life. If you want to go to a romantic movie, try out a new restaurant, or travel to a new country, do it. Find a friend to join you or do it alone. Life does not have to stop while you wait for someone to share it with. When you take risks, do new things, and travel to new places, you learn more about yourself and you may meet someone new.

Try to focus on loving yourself and taking care of yourself. Don't worry about what other people think about you or whether you'll ever meet the right person. You should be happy with yourself first before you can really be happy with someone else. You want to be happy together and not have to rely on someone to make you happy.

Also, give yourself a round of applause and pat on the back for getting to this point in your life by yourself. You did it. You're living your life, you're paying your own bills, you're solving your own problems. I think you're awesome and amazing. I want you to know you're not alone; there are a lot of us out there. Stay true to yourself and be positive. No matter what, the best is yet to come if you let it. Most importantly, always remember (no matter how many bad dates or questions)   to   keep   loving   yourself.

Index of Guys

1 | Elementary/Junior High School

- LilBowWowWannabe

2 | High School

- Mr. Wimpity-WimpWimp
- MyPrecious
- TheNextDoorNeighbor

3 | College

- Mr. FirstNightOfCollege
- Mr. TooMuchTooSoon
- MyPrecious
- Mr. Italiano
- TheHighSchoolGuyAtARandomCollegeParty
- TheNextDoorNeighbor
- Mr. TheFeelingWasn'tThere
- Mr. Norwegian
- TheOneWhoShowsYouHowYouShouldBeTreated
- Mr. FakeFacebookRelationship
- Mr. SmoothTalker
- TheOneYourFamilyWantsYouToMarry

4 | Grad School

- TheNextDoorNeighbor

- TheTexan
- TheBrazilianFighterPilot
- Mr. I'mAChangedMan
- TheFriendWhoNeverKnewILikedHim

5 | Adult Life

- TheOneYourFriendRecommends
- Mr. LiarLiarPantsOnFire
- TheFriendWhoNeverKnewILikedHim
- TheOneYouMeetWhenYou'reNotLooking
- TheWeddingDate
- TheMuchOlderMan
- TheOne

My Thank Yous

Thank you to all the men who I've met and dated in my life, without you I would have never written this book. Thank you to all the people who have questioned me about my dating life, you gave me the motivation and passion to write about my experiences in hopes of changing your opinion of single people.

Thank you to my mom and dad who always support me and want the best for me. Thank you for dealing with my emotional rants about my dating life. Thank you for always believing in me and showing me I am enough. An extra thank you to my mom who spent time reading, editing, and giving me helpful feedback.

Thank you to my sister, Katie Campbell, and my brother, Alex Rodabaugh, for helping me with my podcast and always supporting my passions.

Thank you to my friends who haven't been single for long, but always supported me and tried to understand. Thank you to one of those friends, Paola Seguil, who helped me with edits and improvements to my book.

Thank you to Colton Bowshier for helping me create a killer cover and author photo. Thank you to Nina Denison for her editing magic that helped my book read even better.

Thank you to Ellie Ewing for always believing in me from the beginning (three years ago) and being the first to give me feedback as I just started to write.

Thank you to Emily Valandingham for always supporting me and commiserating with me on all those bad dates.

Thank you to my friend Katharine Dean, who on short notice read my book and helped make it even better. Also thank you to her and my mom for the idea to add book club questions.

Finally, I want to thank YOU for buying my book and reading it! You seriously rock! Please share with your friends! I hope this book changes your opinion about modern dating and helps you see single people in a whole new light.

Book Club Questions

1. In the seventh grade, Ashley asked out LilBowWowWannabe and he rejected her. She was made fun of at school for it. Have you ever asked someone on a date and they rejected you? How did you handle the rejection? How did it make you feel? If you haven't, how do you think it would've impacted your dating life if it had happened to you?

2. In high school, Ashley was asked out and broken up with online. Have you ever started a relationship online? Do you think the internet has helped or hurt relationships? Why or why not?

3. In high school, Ashley's boyfriend MyPrecious surprised her with a one-month anniversary gift. Have you ever celebrated such milestones in a relationship? How did you celebrate?

What was the best anniversary gift you received from a significant other?

4. The subtitle for the college chapter is the Mrs. degree. Have you ever heard of the Mrs. degree before this book? Did you know girls who only attended college with the goal of finding a man to marry? What is your opinion of the Mrs. degree?

5. In college, Ashley meets Mr. TooMuch-TooSoon and his creation of a Facebook relationship status caused her a lot of anxiety. Have you ever met someone who you weren't ready to date? Have you ever had anxiety about posting pictures or publicizing your relationship on social media? Have you seen the public demise of a relationship on social media? Have you wished your relationship was like others who post a lot about how they have the best relationship ever? Do you think people who constantly post about their relationships on social media are accurately depicting their relationship?

6. In college Ashley had a roommate (SisterWho-WantsMyMister) who succeeded in causing tension between her and a guy. Has anyone ever interfered with her relationship? Have

you ever interfered with someone else's relationship?

7. In grad school, Ashley met a foreigner and connected with him immediately. Have you ever met someone and made what you thought was a deep connection the instant you met? Did your relationship continue after meeting or end? If you haven't, do you wish you could've had this experience?

8. In the Adult world, Ashley tries online dating apps. Have you ever gone on a date with someone you met on a dating app? Which app is your favorite? If you've never gone on a dating app date, do you wish it had been available before you met your significant other? Have you ever viewed dating apps as a game? Have you ever met someone on a dating app who was in a relationship or messaged you for days but never met up with you? Do you think dating apps are good or bad? Why?

9. Share a story of your worst date.

10. Ashley finally met TheOne. How did her meeting him make you feel? Have you had a similar experience?

11. Have you felt any pressure to have a relationship by family, friends or coworkers? Have you stayed in a relationship just so you wouldn't have to be single? Have you ever pressured your friends or family about their relationship status?

12. What is the longest amount of time you've been single? What were the pros and cons of not being in a relationship?

13. Throughout the book Ashley talks about the unsolicited advice (i.e., try online dating, don't try too hard) she received from others. Have you ever received advice about dating? What is the worst and best advice you've received?

14. Most of the guys broke up with Ashley. Have you ever had someone end your relationship? How did that make you feel? What, if any, impact did it have on your future relationships? If you've never had someone end a relationship, how do you think it would have changed your dating life?

15. Have you ever questioned why/how someone you know could still be single? Did this book help you understand how it can be harder for some people to find a significant other? Why

or why not? Did it leave you with more questions? What are those questions?

Made in the USA
Monee, IL
05 March 2020

22764033R00173